Highly RECOMMENDED

English for the Hotel and Catering Industry

Rod Revell & Trish Stott

Oxford University Press

Oxford University Press
Walton Street, Oxford OX2 6DP

Oxford New York Toronto
Delhi Bombay Calcutta Madras Karachi
Petaling Jaya Singapore Hong Kong Tokyo
Nairobi Dar es Salaam Cape Town
Melbourne Auckland

and associated companies in
Berlin Ibadan

Oxford, Oxford English and the *Oxford English
logo* are trade marks of Oxford University Press

ISBN 0 19 437648 6

© Oxford University Press 1988

First published 1988
Second impression 1989

Phototypeset in News Gothic and
Palatino by Tradespools Ltd.

Printed in Hong Kong

ACKNOWLEDGEMENTS

The authors and publisher would like to thank the following
for their advice and assistance in the preparation of this
course:

The teaching staffs of the:

Lycée Technique Hôtelier, Guyancourt
LEP Conflans Ste. Honorine, Paris
LEP Edmond Rostand, Paris
LEP Jean Quarré, Paris
LEP Parc Montaleau, Sucy-en-Brie

Simone Fehlmann, Inspectrice de l'Enseignement Technique,
Académie de Caen
Janette Samuel, Professeur et chercheur en éducation
Rosa Hall
M. Moreau

Ashley de Safrin, Novotel/Mercure/Sofitel Group
Athenaeum Hotel, London
15 North Parade, Oxford
H. Brandt, Hotel Majestic, Cannes
Complete Kitchen Equipment Ltd, Oxford
French Tourist Office, London
Grape Ideas, Oxford
Le Petit Blanc, Oxford
Le Café Francais, Headington, Oxford
Le Manoir aux Quatre Saisons, Great Milton
Linton Lodge, Oxford
Oxford College of Further Education
Salisburys, Oxford
Spanish Tourist Office, London
The Randolph Hotel, Oxford
The Duke of Cambridge, Oxford
The Post House, Heathrow
Viking Hotel, York
Whately Hall Hotel, Banbury
York College of Arts and Technology: Dept. of
Community Studies

For permission to reproduce photographs:

Anthony Blake Photo Library   Picturepoint
Art Directors   Robert Harding
BBC Hulton Picture Library   Susan Griggs
London Regional Transport   Trust House Forte

Illustrations by:

John Bendall   Vanessa Luff
Andy Bylo   Hilary Saville
Helen Charlton   Kate Simpson
Antonia Enthoven   Hany Tamba
Kevin Jones & Associates   Paul Thomas

Location and studio photography by:

Martyn Chillmaid   Rob Judges   Mark Mason

Food prepared and arranged by Wendy Veal

TEACHER'S INTRODUCTION

Aims of the course

Highly Recommended is designed to improve the job-related English of people who are training for, or who have already started, careers in hotel and catering. The functional aspects of the course describe the work routines of the following personnel: receptionists, porters, maids, doormen, waiters, waitresses and bar and kitchen staff. These work routines demonstrate a range of skills needed in a great variety of situations where employees have to use English with both customers and other members of staff.

Entry level

The course is intended for learners at the false beginner level in English.

Method of use

The course is designed for use in a class setting with a teacher. Each unit has material which is useful for self-study or homework purposes.

Parts of the course

This book and a cassette which contains two listening activities for each of the 28 units.
The Teacher's Book contains the Answer Key. The Student's edition is without Key.

Structure of the course

The course consists of 28 units which take the student, in functional sequence, through a number of hotel and restaurant routines, beginning with phoned enquiries and reservations, and ending with payment of bills, queries and farewells. As well as its functional aspect each unit identifies particular language areas for study and a number of key expressions have been highlighted. The Contents Chart summarises this.

The units are divided into these sections:

Listening 1 demonstrates the title of the unit in a dialogue or series of dialogues with comprehension checks.

Language Study isolates key expressions, explains language structures and provides grammar exercises. It then lists alphabetically the new words of the unit. There is a multi-lingual word list at the back of the book in English, French, Italian, Spanish, German, and Greek which includes all the new words in the Language Study sections.

Listening 2 expands the theme of the unit and provides further listening and speaking practice. The classroom tasks are often spoken pairwork.

Activity: a lighthearted activity such as a puzzle or word search can be completed in class or as homework.

A brief recap of what has been covered in the unit is given in the *Summary*. This is followed by *Extra Words* which are there to stimulate the students and to provide material for teachers faced with classes of learners at different language levels.

Classroom use

The course has been designed to provide material for a one year job-specific language course in which the students spend approximately 2 hours per week learning English. The amount of time spent on each unit will of course vary depending on the language level of learners, their knowledge of the professional background, the amount of work done as homework and individual adaptation by teachers.

An extensive Answer Key is provided which includes pedagogic notes concerning irregularities and model answers for some exercises. It is recommended that teachers check the Key and pre-teach irregularities before doing the exercises.

The Language Study covers a number of basic grammar structures but does not attempt to be exhaustive on these. A simple grammar reference book with supplementary exercises such as Eastwood & Mackin's 'A Basic English Grammar', OUP 1986, would be a useful classroom resource.

These notes on how to use the course are intended only as a guide. Teachers will find it necessary to adapt to the needs of their students.

Listening 1

Introduce students to the theme of the unit and briefly introduce the listening dialogue. Play through without stopping. Discuss dialogues and clear up any misunderstandings. Students may need to refer to the word list at the back of the book. Play dialogues again as necessary so that students can do the comprehension check as they listen. Go over the answers together. The script of the dialogues is at the back of the book. Encourage students *not* to look at the script before listening.

Language Study

Ask students to read the Expressions aloud and to make complete sentences where necessary using the information in the dialogues.

You will notice that the small squares before the expressions vary in colour. This indicates who is more likely to use the expression: the member of staff or the guest.

  guest/customer speaking to staff;

  staff speaking to guest/customer;

  either guest or member of staff.

Introduce the main points of the Structures to Practice, explain the examples and any possible irregularities and go through the exercises together using as many of the New Words as possible. Finally, check that the meanings and pronunciation of all words are known.

Listening 2

Play the dialogues as many times as is necessary for students to be able to carry out the task in this section. Encourage students to pay attention to pronunciation and intonation in oral exercises.

Activity

Can be pursued individually or in pairs or small groups. Solutions to the activities can be compared in class.

Extra Words

The different categories of Extra Words are listed in Appendix 2.

Students should find out the meanings and pronunciation of these new words by using their own dictionaries and then checking with the teacher.

There are numerous ways of making vocabulary learning an interesting task. Particularly useful is a book by John Morgan and Mario Rinvolucri called 'Vocabulary' in the 'Oxford Resource Books for Teachers Series', OUP 1986.

CONTENTS

UNIT CONTENTS CHART

UNIT	COMMUNICATIVE AREA	TOPIC/SITUATION	STRUCTURES	EXPRESSIONS
1	Taking phone calls	Incoming hotel and restaurant calls.	Simple questions with *can, could, who, what*.	Can I help you? Can/could I have . . . ? I'd like to . . . Who's calling? What name, please?
2	Giving information	Hotel and restaurant location, facilities & prices. Identifying yourself.	Simple Present of *be*. *There is/are*.	The hotel is in . . . There's a . . . There are two . . . I'm Mrs . . . My name's Mr . . .
3	Taking reservations	Opening and closing times.	Questions using *is/are; do/does*. *How many?* *from/to/on/at* *When?*	What time do you . . . ? Are you open . . . ? From 12.00 to 2.30. How many for? What names?
4	Apologizing	Turning down reservations.	Short forms of *be/do/have*.	I'm sorry, we're . . . I'm afraid we haven't. I'm sorry, we don't.
5	Receiving guests	Guests arriving at hotel reception and at restaurant.	Possessive adjectives: *my/ your/his/her/its; our/your/ their*. Questions on days and dates.	Here's your . . . Come this way, please. I'll show you to your . . . Can I take your coats? What day is the tenth?
6	Polite requests and responses	In the bar.	Questions using *may/can/ would/shall/could*.	Would you like . . . What can I get you? May I . . . ? Shall I . . . ?
7	Instructions	Mixing a cocktail.	Imperatives: *take/fill/pour*. Adverbs of time and frequency.	First take a glass. Then fill it with . . . Finally give it a . . . Always put in a . . .
8	Asking for information	Restaurants – taking orders for aperitifs and starters.	*a/the* *a/some*	Would you like an . . . ? Here are the . . . Can we have some . . . ? Do you have a . . . ?

Unit Contents Chart

UNIT	COMMUNICATIVE AREA	TOPIC/SITUATION	STRUCTURES	EXPRESSIONS
9	Asking and explaining	Restaurant – taking orders for main courses.	*How?* *some/any*	It's a kind of . . . We haven't any . . . I'm afraid . . . but . . . How would you like . . .? I'll have some . . .
10	Asking and comparing	Restaurant – wine waiter taking orders.	*Which?* comparing: *–er than, more . . . than, not as . . . as*	Which is . . . X or Y? X is . . . than Y. Which do you prefer?
11	Presenting information	Restaurant – for cheese/dessert/ coffee.	Formal questions with *could, may, would.* Less formal with *can, do.* *on/in/with*	I'm glad you enjoyed it. Would you like . . .? What have you got? What about . . .?
12	Recommending	Restaurant – advising guests on wines.	Positive and Comparative adjectives.	It's very good. I can recommend . . . It's quite dry. Have you tried . . .? May I suggest . . .?
13	Dealing with requests	Requests for items in restaurants.	*I'll* *some/one/another/some more*	I'll get one/some. I'll get another. I'll be right with you. What kind would you like?
14	Describing food dishes	Chef going through menu with trainee.	Simple Present and Simple Present passive for description.	It consists of . . . It contains . . . It's made from . . .
15	Dealing with complaints (1)	Guests complaining in a restaurant.	Simple Past. Superlative adjectives: *worst, most expensive.*	We ordered 20 minutes ago. I'm very sorry. I asked for it rare. I'll change it for you. My apologies sir.
16	Describing jobs and workplaces	Kitchen – a head chef showing a new commis around.	*This/these/here* *That/those/there.* More prepositions.	He's responsible for . . . This is your station. Those are the heat lamps. They are kept here . . .

UNIT	COMMUNICATIVE AREA	TOPIC/SITUATION	STRUCTURES	EXPRESSIONS
17	Explaining and instructing	The chef going over cooking methods with a new commis.	*Why? . . . Because . . .* Must/have to/don't have to/mustn't.	*First we have to . . . What's this for? I'll see to . . . That's the lot. Is that it? You mustn't do it quickly.*
18	Taking an order on the phone	Hotel room service – a guest ordering breakfast.	Adverbs. *either . . . or . . . both*	One moment, I'll put you through. Am I too late . . .? There's either . . . or . . . Both, please. Anything else, madam?
19	Asking for clarification	Hotel reception – reservations by phone.	Simple Past: questions and negative statements.	We seem to have a bad line. Can you speak up? Could you spell that? I'm sorry, I didn't catch that. Excuse me, . . .? We'll hold the rooms until . . .
20	Dealing with phoned requests	Hotel facilities and services.	*Need/don't need/needn't.*	My jacket needs . . . Somebody'll pick it up. I need some . . . You needn't . . . I don't need them until . . . I'll send someone up.
21	Giving directions indoors	Hall Porter and chambermaid to guests.	Direction and location prepositions.	It's on the . . . Take the lift to . . . Walk along the corridor. Go down the corridor. Go through . . . Go past . . . Go across . . .
22	Giving directions outside	Hall Porter and doorman directing guests in a city.	More prepositions.	Is it far? No, not far. About 10 minutes' walk. Turn left outside . . . Go down to the . . . Go straight on . . .

Unit Contents Chart

UNIT	COMMUNICATIVE AREA	TOPIC/SITUATION	STRUCTURES	EXPRESSIONS
23	Offering help and advice	Hall Porter to guests.	Present Perfect with *yet*, *just*. *may/might* *ought to/should*	What have you planned? Have you heard anything? You ought to go to . . . I believe it's very good. I'll send the porter out . . . I'll phone the . . . for you.
24	Dealing with complaints (2)	Hotel – guests to reception.	*should have . . ./should have been . . .*	My room hasn't been cleaned. It should've been done. The noise next door is awful. I'll speak to . . .
25	Paying bills	Hotel and restaurant – payments.	Object pronouns. Present Continuous.	How are you paying? Service and tax are included. Would you sign here, please? I'll stamp it for you. Here's your receipt. Do you have a banker's card?
26	Payment queries	Hotel and restaurant – guests query bills with reception and waiter.	*Much/many/a lot of*	It can't be right. I'll check it for you. I'm afraid there's no mistake. I beg your pardon, that's our mistake.
27	Farewells	Hotel and restaurant – guests are leaving.	Future reference.	I hope you enjoyed your stay. We're flying to . . . today. We're going to see . . . This looks like your taxi. I hope we'll see you again. Have a pleasant trip. Safe journey.
28	Answering personal questions	A job interview.	Letter: beginnings and endings.	Dear Sir/Madam, Yours faithfully, Dear Mr/Mrs/Miss/Ms, Yours sincerely, With reference to . . . I enclose . . .

Listening one

Listen to the four telephone calls and put in the missing words.

Language study

Expressions to learn

- Can I help you?
- Who's calling?
- What name, please?
- Can I have . . . ?
- Could I have . . . ?
- Could I speak to . . . ?
- I'd like to . . .

Structures to practise

Making simple questions with **can** and **could**, **who** and **what**.

Expand these notes into sentences, as in this example:
morning/help
▶ *Good morning, can I help you?*

1 afternoon/help
2 double room/4 nights
3 table for 5/Tuesday
4 yes/name
5 speak/manager
6 single room/Monday–Thursday
7 yes/who
8 table for 2/Saturday/8pm

New words to use

Check the meaning of these new words in the Glossary at the back of this book.

book	manager	number	table
double	name	reserve	
full	night	single	

Listening two

Listen to the dialogue. In what order do these words come?

1 table	4 evening	7 help	10 restaurant
2 single	5 name	8 Saturday	
3 reserve	6 book	9 nights	

Activity

Find the missing words. Use them to fill in the crossword:

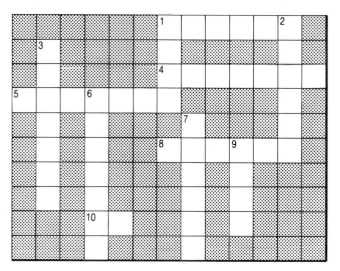

Across →

1 A room for four
   _____, please. (4–8 August)
4 Good _____.
5 Could I _____ a table for two, please?
8 A room for two.
10 __, I'm sorry, the hotel is full.

Down ↓

1 My ____ is Jose Artesco.
2 A room for one person.
3 The day before Wednesday.
6 Good _____.
7 The day after Sunday.
9 Can I ____ a room, please?

Summary

Now you can
Answer the telephone politely
Good morning, can I help you?

Ask for things
Can I have your name, please?

Say what you want
I'd like a single room.

Ask who is on the phone
Who's calling?

• E X T R A • W O R D S •

These words are *not* in the Glossary. Use your dictionary to check the meanings.

days of the week	numbers	greetings	room types
Monday	one	Good morning	single
Tuesday	two	Good afternoon	double
Wednesday	three	Good evening	twin
Thursday	four		family
Friday	five		suite
Saturday	six		
Sunday	seven		
	eight		
	nine		
	ten		

1

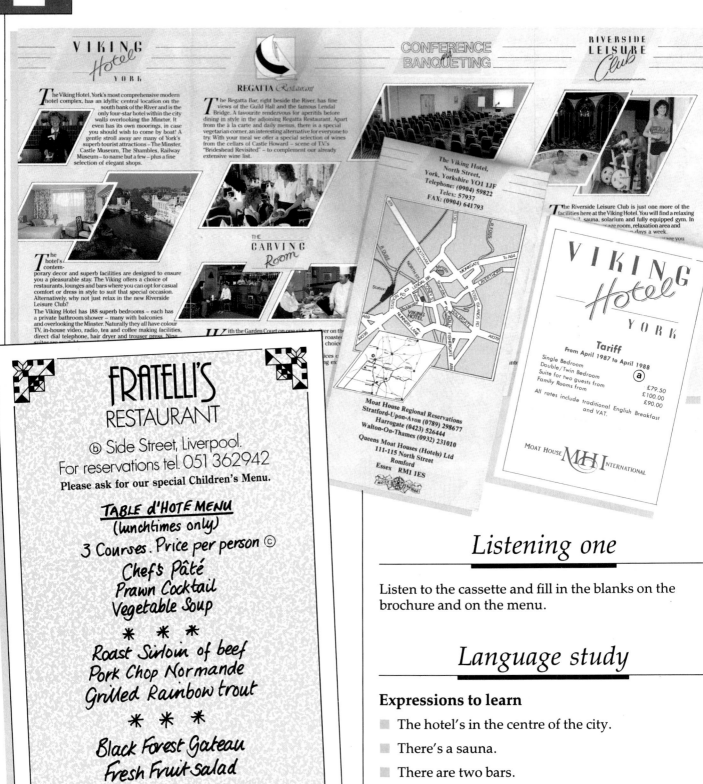

Listening one

Listen to the cassette and fill in the blanks on the brochure and on the menu.

Language study

Expressions to learn

- The hotel's in the centre of the city.
- There's a sauna.
- There are two bars.
- The cost is £16.50.
- I'm Mr Evans.
- My name's Evans.

Structures to practise

Describing things using the Present tense of the verb **to be** and using **there is/there are**.

This table shows the full and short forms:

Singular		Plural	
I am	I'm	We are	We're
You are	You're	You are	You're
He is	He's		
She is	She's	They are	They're
It is	It's		
There is	There's	There are	There are

Remember: **There is** a sauna.   **There's** a sauna.
There are two bars.   **There are** two bars.

Fill in the blanks. Use short forms where possible:

I (1) ..... the manager of the Savoy Hotel. My name (2) ..... Mr Black. The hotel (3) ..... in Main Street. There (4) ..... 100 double rooms and 20 single rooms. (5) ..... a bar and a restaurant. There (6) ..... table d'hôte meals at lunchtime and table d'hôte and à la carte in the evening.

New words to use

Check the meaning of these new words in the Glossary at the back of this book.

à la carte	exchange	per
bar	exit	sauna
car park	handicap facilities	special
centre	information	street
city	meal	swimming-pool
coffee shop	men's toilet	table d'hôte
course	menu	women's toilet

Listening two

Listen to the cassette. What are the people talking about and how much does it cost?

Activity

Look at these twelve symbols and decide which word goes with each. Check the meanings in the Glossary if you need to.

1 restaurant	5 exchange	9 telephone
2 handicap facilities	6 women	10 exit
3 car park	7 toilets	11 coffee shop
4 swimming-pool	8 men	12 information

Summary

Now you can
Identify yourself
I'm Peter.
My name's Evans.

Talk about numbers
There are 27 rooms.

Say where you are
The hotel's in Park Street.
The restaurant's at 23 Green Street.

Talk about prices
The cost is . . .
The price is . . .

• E X T R A • W O R D S •

These words are *not* in the Glossary. Use your dictionary to check the meanings.

currencies	numbers	
Pounds	eleven	twenty
Dollars	twelve	thirty
Francs	thirteen	forty
Marks	fourteen	fifty
Crowns	fifteen	sixty
Yen	sixteen	seventy
Pesetas	seventeen	eighty
	eighteen	ninety
	nineteen	a hundred

2

3

MEMO

Dino's for lunch

opens ① . . . .
closes ② . . . .
closed on ③ . . . .

DINO'S RESTAURANT

Table Reservations   WEEK No.
                            18

Day: ④ ——————
Number of people: ⑤ ——————
Time: ⑥ ——————
Name: ⑦ ——————

Listening one

Listen and fill in the information on the note pads.

Language study

Expressions to learn

▓ What time do you serve lunch?

▓ Are you open every day?

▓ from Tuesday to Sunday

▓ on Monday

▓ at 1pm

▓ What name is it?

▓ How many for?

Structures to practise

Questions and answers in the Simple Present tense are for routines, timetables, and the everyday state of things.

Making questions using **is** and **are**
Is it . . . ? Is there . . . ?
Are you . . . ? Are there . . . ?

Making questions using **do**
Do you serve . . . ?
Does he speak . . . ?

Work in pairs. Ask questions and give answers for the following information. Then write them down.

Example:
time/lunch ▶ *What time do you serve lunch?*
12.30–2.00 ▶ *We serve lunch from 12.30 to 2.00.*

1 open/every day?
  closed/Mondays
2 time/dinner?
  7–11
3 table for 6/Saturday lunch
  yes/time?
4 open/evening?
  seven o'clock
5 have/single room/Friday?
  certainly/name?

New words to use

am	every day	leave	pm
close	get up	lunch	room
closed	go	o'clock	serve
do	head waiter	open	travel

Listening two

Listen to people talking about the time.

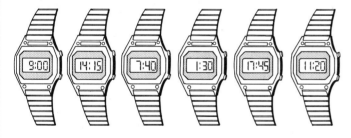

Now write in the times in the displays yourself:

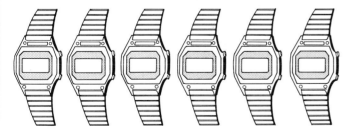

Activity

Work in pairs. Ask and answer questions about your routines.

What time do you   get up?
                        have breakfast?
                        leave your home?

How do you   travel to school/college?
What time do you   have lunch?
                        go home?

What do you   do in the evening?
etc . . .

Summary

Now you can
Ask time questions
What time do you open?

Answer time questions
We open at 6.

Ask other questions
How many rooms do you want?

Talk about the time
I get up at 7.30.

• E X T R A • W O R D S •

seasons	restaurant staff	titles	meals
winter	Maître d'hôtel	Mr	breakfast
spring	Maître d'accueil	Ms	lunch
summer	Maître d'	Mrs	dinner
autumn	Head Waiter	Miss	
	Wine Waiter		
	waitress		
	waiter		

3

Listening

As you listen, answer the question word under each picture.

For example: **1** when? ▶ *for tonight*

Language study

Expressions to learn

- I'm sorry, we're fully booked.
- I'm afraid we haven't any left.
- I'm very sorry, we don't open on Sundays.
- We've nothing left.
- I'm sorry, there's no answer.

Structures to practise

In spoken English, and informal written English, we usually use the short forms (contractions) of the verbs **be**, **have** and **do**.

Short forms

Be			
I'm	I'm not	we're	we aren't
you're	you aren't	you're	you aren't
he's	he isn't		
she's	she isn't	they're	they aren't
it's	it isn't		

Have			
I've	I haven't	we've	we haven't
you've	you haven't	you've	you haven't
he's	he hasn't		
she's	she hasn't	they've	they haven't
it's	it hasn't		

Do			
I do	I don't	we do	we don't
you do	you don't	you do	you don't
he does	he doesn't		
she does	she doesn't	they do	they don't
it does	it doesn't		

Use the short forms in these sentences. Say them, then write them down.
1 We are open six days per week.
2 We do not open on Mondays.
3 I am afraid we do not have any rooms tonight.
4 I am sorry, he is not here.
5 I am afraid we have not any tables left for Friday night.
6 It is a very busy night.
7 We do not serve lunch before 12 o'clock.
8 They have not left a message.
9 They are open every evening.
10 She does not have lunch at home.

New words to use

answer   fully booked   nothing   tonight
busy   message   tomorrow

Listening two

Listen to the cassette and note down all the numbers, prices, days and times.

Activity

Ask questions and give answers about these pictures:

Summary

Now you can
Use the short forms of **be, have** and **do**
I'm sorry, we're closed.
They don't have any rooms.
She hasn't left a message.

Apologize
I'm afraid we haven't any . . .
I'm sorry, he isn't here.

• E X T R A • W O R D S •

holidays	the year	the day
Christmas	week	today
New Year	weekend	this morning
Easter	month	this afternoon
Whitsun	year	this evening

5

Listening one

Listen to the cassette and decide what the objects and people numbered 1 to 12 are.

1	7
2	8
3	9
4	10
5	11
6	12

Language study

Expressions to learn

- Could you fill in this . . . ?
- Here's your . . .
- Do you want . . . ?
- Come this way.
- I'll show you to your table.

Structures to practise

The possessive adjective refers to the possessor, not the thing possessed. It remains the same whether the thing possessed is singular or plural.
Example: **my** bag; **my** bags

Possessive adjectives

my	our
your	your
his her its	their

A Use possessive adjectives in the blanks below.
Example: *I enjoy* **my** *job.*

1 He wants some help with . . . luggage.
2 They want to put . . . car in the car park.
3 We prefer to have breakfast in . . . room.
4 She wants to leave . . . coat.
5 I'd like to leave a message for . . . friend.

B Now change these sentences into questions offering help. Use the polite form 'Would you like . . .?'
Example: 1 *Would you like some help with your luggage?*

New words to use

car	floor	luggage	receptionist
coat	guest	porter	registration card
date of birth	key	prefer	restaurant diary
fill in	key card		

Listening two

Listen to the cassette and answer the questions using this calendar page:

APRIL 1988

M	T	W	T	F	S	S
—	—	—	—	1	2	3
4	5	6	7	8	9	10
11	12	13	14	15	16	17
18	19	20	21	22	23	24
25	26	27	28	29	30	—

Now practise asking questions and giving dates with a partner.

Activity

Work in pairs. Ask for, and give, personal information for this hotel registration card. Student A has information on page 103 and student B on page 104.

HOTEL PLAZA

REGISTRATION CARD
Name _____
First Names _____
Nationality _____

Home Address
_____
_____

FREE RESERVATION SERVICE
Travelling on to other places in the U.K. & Europe?
Please ask the receptionist if we can help make your reservation

Signature _____

FOREIGN VISITORS
Passport Number
_____
Date and Place of Issue
_____
Next Address
_____
_____
_____

Room No.	No. of Persons	Charge	Date of Arrival	No. of Nights or Departure Date

Summary

Now you can
Ask questions about days and dates
Is the fourth a Friday?

Talk about who something belongs to
It's their car.

• EXTRA • WORDS •

numbers (ordinal)		months	
first	tenth	January	July
second	eleventh	February	August
third	twelfth	March	September
fourth	thirteenth	April	October
fifth	fourteenth	May	November
sixth	fifteenth	June	December
seventh	sixteenth		
eighth	twentieth		
ninth	thirtieth		

5

whisky

dry martini

cider

dry sherry

gin and tonic

beer

brandy

red wine

Listening one

Guests are ordering their drinks in the bar. What do they order?

Tim	
Denise	
Michael	
Jill	

Language study

Expressions to learn

- What can I get you?
- What would you like?
- Would you like ice?
- What'll you have?
- Shall I charge this to your room?
- May I have your key card, please?

Structures to practise

Could/would/may and **shall** are polite forms:

Could I have a beer? **May I** have your key card? **Would you** like ice?	very polite/formal
What'll you have? (will) **Can I** have my key?	less formal
Shall I charge this to you?	requesting permission politely or offering a service

In pairs, as guest and barman, order drinks using the words to help you. (Remember: *sweet **or** dry*)
Example:
gin and tonic ▶ Guest: *Can I have a gin and tonic?*
ice and lemon ▶ Barman: *Would you like ice and lemon?*

1 sherry
   sweet/dry
	3 port
	   small/large
		5 lager
		   draught/bottled

2 beer
   pint/half
	4 whisky
	   water/soda
		6 vodka and tonic
		   ice

New words to use

bitter	draught	lager	rum	tonic
bottled	dry	large	sherry	whisky
charge	gin	lemon	small	wine
cider	half	pint	soda	
drinks	ice	port	sweet	

Listening Two

Listen to the 5 people on the cassette. They are buying drinks for their friends. How much do you charge each person? The prices are in pence. There are 100 pence in each pound.

	pint/half	
Beer *(bitter)*	90	45
Beer *(lager)*	96	48
Cider	80	40

	large/small	
Whisky	130	65
Vodka	120	60
Gin	120	60
Rum	120	60
Lemonade	40	20
Tonic	40	20

Activity

Find the ten drinks in the puzzle below:

B	R	E	T	A	W	F	N
R	V	A	M	H	G	M	O
A	O	G	I	N	V	W	B
N	D	S	N	E	K	O	C
D	K	W	I	N	E	O	Q
Y	A	F	T	Q	G	S	S
C	O	Z	R	N	B	O	W
R	H	C	A	U	V	F	B
K	D	C	M	S	M	L	L

Summary

Now you can
Ask people what they want and take orders for drinks
What can I get you?
I'd like a half of cider, please.

Check with guests if they need a service
Shall I charge this to your room?

• E X T R A • W O R D S •

spirits (hard liquor)	wines (fortified)	wines (table)	mixers
whisky	vermouth	Bordeaux	soda
gin	sherry	Beaujolais	tonic
brandy	port	Chianti	ginger ale
Cognac	Dubonnet	Rioja	coke
pastis	madeira	Mosel	juice
rum	muscatel	Riesling	
vodka		Muscadet	
		Mâcon	
		Barsac	
		Chablis	
		Lambrusco	
		Sancerre	

17

6

Listening one

Listen to the instructions for making a dry martini and then number the pictures in the correct order.

Language study

Expressions to learn

▨ Take a glass

▨ Fill it with ice

▨ Pour in a measure of dry vermouth

▨ Add two measures of dry gin

▨ first/next/then/finally

▨ always/often/sometimes/rarely/never

▨ Give it a good shake/stir

Structures to practise

Short sentences beginning with imperatives like **Take, Fill** and **Pour** are used for giving instructions.

A Describe how you:
1 make a cup of coffee
2 make a cup of tea
3 make your favourite drink
4 make a telephone call

B Are you the same?
Example: *Yes, I'm the same.* or
         No, I rarely . . .
Maria always has tea at breakfast.
Peter always gets up at 7am.
Annie often works at the weekend.
Mike never drinks beer in the evening.
Gabby rarely drinks a cocktail.
David sometimes has wine with lunch.

New words to use

add	decorate	mix	shake
all right	fill	never	shaker
always	finally	next	slice
bar steward	glass	often	sometimes
below	grenadine	olive	start
broken	ingredients	parasol	stir
chill	lime	pass through	strainer
cocktail	liquid	pour	take
cocktail shaker	make	quarter	throw out
dash	measure	rarely	

Listening two

On the cassette you will hear how two famous cocktails, the Daiquiri and the Manhattan are made. Write down the ingredients and how to make each of them.

Activity

There are seven instructions below for making a cocktail called a 'Broadway'. Put them in the right order.

1 Shake well
2 First put in a dash of orange bitters
3 After the vermouth, add six centilitres of dry gin
4 Pass through a strainer
5 Half fill a shaker with broken ice
6 Serve in a small wine glass
7 Next add three centilitres of Italian vermouth

Summary

Now you can
Ask how to do something
How do you serve a Bloody Mary?

Understand and give instructions
Take a glass and then fill it with ice.

Say how often you do things
I sometimes drink wine with my lunch.

• E X T R A • W O R D S •

fractions	liqueurs	cocktails
quarter	Bailey's Irish	Americano
half	Cream	Bloody Mary
three quarters	Benedictine	Bronx
one fifth	Chartreuse	Harvey Wallbanger
	Cointreau	Pina Colada
	Cuarenta y tres	Tequila Sunrise
	Drambuie	Tom Collins
	Grand Marnier	Whisky Sour
	Sambuca	
	Strega	
	Tia Maria	

7

TO START

Soup of the day	£ 1.50
Grilled sardines	2.00
Avocado with prawns	2.50
Melon with Parma ham	2.50
Pâté Maison	2.50
Mixed hors d'oeuvres	2.00
Tomato salad	1.75

Listening one

Listen to the cassette and then answer the comprehension questions.

Comprehension check

1 What does the waiter bring the guests?
2 What drink does the man order?
3 What drink does the woman order?
4 What is the soup of the day?
5 Does the woman order it?
6 What does the man order as a starter?
7 What extra order does he ask for?

Language study

Expressions to learn

▓ Can I take your coats?

▓ Are you ready to order?

▓ Here are the menu and wine list.

▓ Would you like to order a drink?

▓ What would you like as a starter?

░ Could we have some bread, please?

Structures to practise

Use **the** for a particular named item and **a** for a non-particular named item. **A** means 'one' and is for countable nouns. Use **some** for uncountables.

A/the

*I'd like **a** beer*. (but: *I'd like **an** aperitif*. Use **an** before vowels)
***The** beer is good*. (the beer I'm drinking)

Fill in the blanks with **a** or **the**:
1 . . . hotel is in . . . city centre.
2 Would you like . . . aperitif?
3 Here is . . . menu.
4 Can I have . . . dry martini, please?
5 Do you have . . . reservation?
6 Could we have . . . wine list?

A/some

*I'd like **a** glass/two beers/three soups* (countable)
*I'd like **some** bread/**some** water* (uncountable)

Check your word lists for uncountable nouns: make a list of them.

New words to use

avocado pear	ham	soup of the day
bread	melon	starter
bottle	mushroom	still
extra	order	stuffed
food	prawn	window
grilled	ready	wine list

Listening two

Listen to orders being taken and note them down.

Activity

You are a waiter/waitress. Ask if your customer wants what is in the pictures.
Would you like | a . . . ?
                   | the . . . ?
                   | some . . . ?

Example:

*Would you like **some** wine?*
or
*Would you like **a** glass of wine?*

Summary

Now you can
Help guests when they arrive
Can I take your coats?
Here is the menu.

Help guests order
Are you ready to order?
Would you like an aperitif/a starter?

Use countable and uncountable words correctly
Two bottles of wine; some bread; a beer.

• E X T R A • W O R D S •

starters	aperitifs
tomato salad	champagne
cucumber salad	kir
mixed salad	Dubonnet
egg mayonnaise	Martini
smoked salmon	St Raphael
mussels in white wine	pastis
salami	Cinzano bitter

9

MAIN COURSES

Sole Meunière	£ 6.95
Turbot in white wine	5.95
Deep fried scampi Béarnaise with rice	5.95
Roast duckling with orange sauce	6.95
Escalope of veal	4.95
Moussaka	4.50
Coq-au-vin	4.75
Grilled steaks Rump	5.95
Fillet	6.95

SIDE DISHES

Jacket potato	.95	Peas	.50
French fries	.95	Green beans	.60
Duchesse potatoes	1.00	Spinach	.75
Cauliflower au		Mushrooms	.95
gratin	1.20	Side salad	1.20

A	Man	E	
B	Woman	F	
C		G	
D		H	
TABLE No.	26	DATE	21/8

A 1 Mixed hors d'œuvres
B 1 Melon, Parma ham

WAITER 3MHD

581484

Listening one

What are the two main course orders?

Language study

Expressions to learn

▨ What would you like to follow?

▨ It's a kind of . . .

▨ We haven't any . . .

▨ I'm afraid . . . but . . .

▨ How would you like it cooked?

▨ I'll have some . . .

Structures to practise

A Ask guests how they want food served using the polite form 'How would you like . . . ?'

Look at these sentences:

How would you like your steak? (rare, medium)
▶ *I'd like it rare, please.*

Make similar questions and answers from these:
1 egg (hard- or soft-boiled)
2 jacket potato (with butter or sour cream)
3 egg (turned over or sunny side up)
4 coffee (black or white)
5 salad (French dressing or mayonnaise)

22

B Some/any
Use **some** with affirmative verbs, **any** with negatives and questions. But for questions with polite forms, e.g. 'Would you . . ?' use **some**.

Look at these sentences. When do you use **some** and when **any**?

1 *I'll have some fish.*
2 *We haven't any sole.*
3 *Do you have any vegetarian dishes?*

Put **some** or **any** in the blanks:
1 I'm afraid we haven't . . . avocados left.
2 I'd like . . . peas, please.
3 They haven't . . . tables free.
4 Do you have . . . tomato soup?
5 Would you like . . . mineral water?
6 Are there . . . staff missing tonight?

C Look at this sentence:
I'm afraid we haven't any sole but the turbot is excellent.

Make similar sentences with 1, 2 and 3.
1 no fillet steak/the rump's very good
2 no pâté de foie gras/the pâté de canard is excellent
3 no cod/the plaice is very good

New words to use

aubergine	fish	plaice	spinach
butter	French fries	rare	staff
cheese	Greek	rice	steak
cod	green beans	rump steak	sunny side up
cooked	hard	sauce	tomato
cream	jacket	scampi	topped
dressing	lamb	settle for	turbot
duckling	medium	side salad	veal
escalope	missing	soft	vegetable
excellent	peas	sole	vegetarian
fillet	pie	sour	

Listening two

Listen to the waiter reading orders to the sous-chef and fill in the table below:

Table number			
Main course(s)			
Vegetables			
Potatoes			

Activity

Using the Extra Words, write descriptions of the main courses on the menu.

Summary

Now you can
Ask customers how they would like their food cooked/served
How would you like your steak?

Explain what different dishes are
Moussaka is a kind of pie with layers of . . .

Use **some** and **any**
We have some soup but we haven't any melon.

Suggest alternatives
I'm afraid we haven't any . . but the . . is very good.

• EXTRA • WORDS •

methods of cooking	vegetables		grilled meat
grill	peas	avocado	blue
(US: broil)	onion	garlic	rare
boil	leek	cabbage	medium rare
roast	carrot	cauliflower	medium
fry	celery	lettuce	well done
poach	asparagus	aubergine	
stew	artichoke	tomato	**types of meat**
bake	Brussels	beans	
steam	sprouts	parsnip	beef
	potato	peppers	pork
	turnip	cucumber	veal
	chicory	mushrooms	lamb
	lentils	watercress	
	radishes		
	fennel		

23

Listening one

Which of these wines are in the dialogue? What do the guests choose?

Language study

Expressions to learn

Which is drier, X or Y?

Would you like something to drink?

Y is sweeter than X.

X is not as dry as Z.

A is more full-bodied than B.

Structures to practise

Compare the use of | . . . er than
| more . . . than
| not as . . . as

Look at these examples:

French wine/+ dry/German wine
▶ *French wine is drier than German wine.*

This Burgundy/+ expensive/that Bordeaux
▶ *This Burgundy is more expensive than that Bordeaux.*

German wine/− dry/French wine
▶ *German wine is not as dry as French wine.*

1 Riesling/+ sweet/Graves
2 A Burgundy bottle/+ fat/a Bordeaux bottle
3 Rosé/− full-bodied/claret
4 Champagne/+ expensive/table wine
5 A Riesling bottle/− narrow/a Burgundy bottle
6 Mineral water/+ cheap/table wine
7 Beaujolais/− expensive/Champagne

New words to use

area	expensive	light	shape
Burgundy	famous	long-necked	sparkling
cheap	fat	narrow	town
claret	fresh	red	white
district	full-bodied		

Listening two

Listen to the wine specialist talking about the wines that come from Portugal, Spain, France and Italy. Identify the regions and wines.

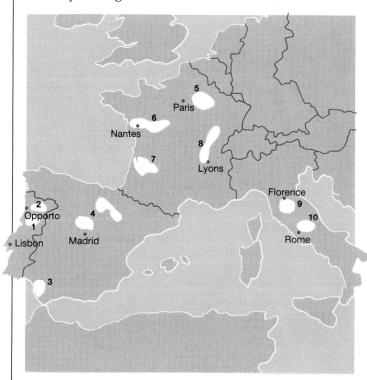

Activity

Fill in the crossword:

Across →	Down ↓
1 You can mix a cocktail in this. (2 words)	1 vegetable
4 in a dry martini	2 drink before a meal
8 very cold	3 popular vegetable in China
10 _____ pear	5 in a dry martini
12 aperitif	6 You go __ reception to check in.
13 fortified ____	7 sort of meat
16 Burgundy is _____ of Lyon.	9 sort of meat
17 vegetable	11 Italian wine
18 from Portugal	14 not __ dry __ Muscadet
19 Strain the dry martini ____ a glass.	15 opposite of cold

Summary

Now you can
Ask guests to choose
Which do you prefer?

Tell guests about the wine
The Barsac is sweet.

Make comparisons
The Barsac is sweeter than the Graves.

Identify some of the important wines
Beaujolais is a red wine from the Burgundy region of eastern France.

• E X T R A • W O R D S •

wine terms	countries and nationalities	directions
cork	France/French	north/northern/ the north of
corkscrew	Belgium/Belgian	
corkage	Spain/Spanish	south/southern/ the south of
label	Italy/Italian	
sediment	Netherlands/Dutch	
vintage	Germany/German	east/eastern/ the east of
a good year for	Denmark/Danish	
château bottled	Sweden/Swedish	
room temperature	Norway/Norwegian	west/western/ the west of
chambré	Greece/Greek	
	Portugal/ Portuguese	
	Switzerland/Swiss	
	Austria/Austrian	

Listening one

List the desserts and cheeses as the waiter presents them. Identify them on the trolley and cheeseboard.

1	7
2	8
3	9
4	10
5	11
6	

Language study

Expressions to learn

- I'm glad you enjoyed it.
- Would you like a dessert?
  - On the top . . .
    - Underneath . . .
    - What have you got?
    - Can you tell us what they are?
    - What about cheese?

Structures to practise

A Use the polite forms **would**, **could** and **may** to guests whenever possible.

> **a Polite formal**
> Could I have . . . ?
> May I suggest the . . . ?
> Would you like . . . ?

> **b Informal**
> Can I get you . . . ?

> **c Informal**
> Do you want . . . ?
> What about a . . . ?

Pair the openers on the left with a phrase on the right. Which scene does each sentence belong in, **a**, **b** or **c**?

1 Would you like . . .   . . . coffee, Bella?
2 Do you want . . .   . . . some more drinks?
3 Could I have . . .   . . . the Graves, sir?
4 Can I get you . . .   . . . to order now, madam?
5 Would you like . . .   . . . your name, please?
6 May I suggest . . .   . . . sparkling or still, madam?

B Fill in the blanks using **on**, **in**, **with**:

on   in   with

1 He put the food . . . the table.
2 She likes biscuits . . . cheese.
3 The wine bottle is . . . the bucket . . . the table.
4 I'd like a green salad . . . my steak.
5 I don't like cream . . . my coffee.

New words to use

basket	chocolate gâteau	piece
biscuits	dessert	profiteroles
bucket	enjoy	sweet
corkscrew	find	top
Charlotte Russe	fruit salad	trolley
cheese board	liqueur	underneath
cheese-cake		

Listening two

Listen to the talk about the cheeses of Europe. What are the three types of cheese? List, for each country, the names of the cheeses.

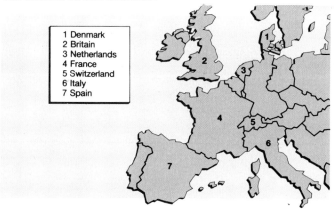

1 Denmark
2 Britain
3 Netherlands
4 France
5 Switzerland
6 Italy
7 Spain

Activity

Work in pairs, one as waiter and one as guest. Use the menus on page 20 (Starters), page 22 (Main Courses), and the pictures in this unit to order meals.

Summary

Now you can
Be sure that you are polite to your guests
Would you like a . . .

Present a dessert trolley to guests
On the top we have . . .

• E X T R A • W O R D S •

fruit

apple	orange	pear	banana
pineapple	lemon	grapefruit	peach
apricot	melon	grape	plum
prune	strawberry	raspberry	blackberry
blueberry	mango	gooseberry	redcurrant
blackcurrant	cherry		

RECOMMENDING

Listening one

List the wines talked about in the dialogue and describe them.

WINE LIST		£
WHITE:	Muscadet de Sèvre et	7.95
	Maine '85	9.65
	Sancerre '84	7.75
	Mâcon Blanc Villages	12.75
	Chablis 84/85	6.75
	Barsac	7.75
	Lambrusco	7.75
	Piesporter Michelsberg	
		9.35
RED:	Fleurie '83	8.95
	Piat de Beaujolais 84/85	6.25
	Mouton Cadet 1983	6.25
	Chianti	6.75
	Rioja Lagunilla 1981	
		6.25
ROSÉ:	Rosé d'Anjou	7.95
	Mateus Rosé	
		15.00
CHAMPAGNE:	Brut	
	Moët et Chandon,	19.25
	Première cuvée	
		5.25
HOUSE WINES:	Medium Red	
per bottle	Medium White	
70cls	Dry White	

Language study

Expressions to learn

- I can recommend the white Bordeaux.
- It's quite dry.
- Have you tried the house wine?
- May I suggest a Burgundy?
- Will that be all?

Structures to practise

Positive and Comparative adjectives
This table shows which words to use with ordinary (positive) adjectives, and which words to use with comparative adjectives.
Notice that **slightly** and **rather** can be used with both.

28

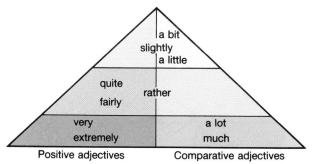

We can *describe* things more precisely like this:
*Dom Perignon is a **very expensive** champagne.*
*Nantes is a **fairly big** city.*
*Try the mild curry. It's **slightly hot**.*

And we can *compare* things more precisely like this:
*Muscatel is **a little** sweeter than Sauternes.*
*Muscatel is **rather** stronger than table wines.*
*Muscatel is **a lot** sweeter than Chablis.*

Now use words from the table to make sentences with the following. In some cases you will be expressing your own opinion.

1 Smoked salmon/tasty/tinned sardines
2 Beer/strong/cider
3 Hotel/busy. Half the rooms are booked.
4 Fillet steak/tender/rump steak
5 Indian food/spicy/American food
6 A good soufflé/difficult to prepare
7 Hotels in provincial towns/cheap/hotels in capital cities
8 French food/good/Italian food (N.B. **good→better**)

New words to use

boiled	ice-cream	probably	smooth	tender
carafe	juicy	quite	spicy	too
fruity	popular	rough	tasty	tough

Listening two

The guide below is not finished. Listen to the people talking and put in three stars ★★★ for 'very good' where they suggest.

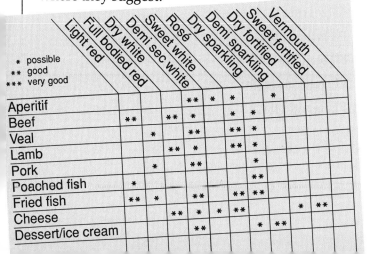

Activity

Find the fifteen food and wine words:

X	S	P	A	R	K	L	I	N	G
F	M	D	K	W	B	X	A	U	R
B	O	I	L	E	D	B	D	U	I
S	O	D	L	P	R	S	R	G	L
D	T	A	S	T	Y	E	V	W	L
Z	H	K	W	A	D	R	A	R	E
F	B	M	E	N	S	X	U	O	D
A	C	D	E	J	L	Q	L	U	B
H	O	T	T	D	S	L	E	G	L
D	L	V	N	E	I	A	X	H	A
S	D	R	W	T	O	U	G	H	M
A	Q	G	S	Y	I	C	M	L	B

Summary

Now you can
Recommend things to guests
I can recommend the . . .

Talk about wines
The Chablis is quite dry.

Suggest the right wine for a type of food
May I suggest the Pouilly Fuissé with the fish?

• E X T R A • W O R D S •

herbs	spices	fish (salt water)	fish (fresh water)
parsley	salt	halibut	trout
thyme	pepper	sea bream	salmon
rosemary	paprika	haddock	pike
sage	mustard	tuna	eel
oregano	chilli pepper	sardines	carp
tarragon		mackerel	perch
marjoram		herring	bream
dill		anchovy	
		mullet	
		red mullet	
		angler fish	
		bass	

12

WAITER, COULD YOU BRING SOME WATER, PLEASE?

WAITER, WE NEED ANOTHER SIDE PLATE.

Listening one

List the ten things that people ask for:

1	6
2	7
3	8
4	9
5	10

Language study

Expressions to learn

▨ I'll get one.

▨ I'll bring some.

▨ I'll be right with you.

▨ I'll get some right away.

▨ I'll be right back.

Structures to practise

Use **some/one/another/some more** instead of repeating the requested item.
Offer your services using **I'll . . .** (I will)

Look at these examples:

I'd like a beer.	*I'll get one.*
I'd like some bread.	*I'll get some.*
This spoon is dirty.	*I'll get another.*
The water jug is empty.	*I'll get some more.*

Respond to the following using **I'll get . . .**
1 There's no pepper on the table.
2 I'd like a glass of water.
3 My fork is on the floor.
4 Can I have an ashtray?
5 Another carafe of house red wine, please.
6 This wine glass is dirty.
7 We've no bread left.

New words to use

above	cover	joint	position
another	dirty	knife	right
ashtray	empty	left	right away
bill	folded	middle	spoon
bring	fork	napkin	water jug
check	get	plate	

Listening two

Listen to the Head Waiter. He is telling a new waiter how to check a cover. Identify the things in the photo as you listen.

Activity

Work in pairs as waiter and guest. Ask for, and offer to bring, the things in the pictures.

Summary

Now you can
Respond to guests' requests
I'll bring some right away.

Understand the items needed on a table
Can I have some pepper and salt?
Certainly, sir.

• E X T R A • W O R D S •

smokers' equipment	poultry	cutlery
cigarettes	chicken	teaspoon
matches	duck	tablespoon
lighter	duckling	
tipped	goose	
non-filter	turkey	
cigars		
pipe		

13

A

B

C

D

E

F

G

H

I

J

K

L

M

N

O

P

DESCRIBING FOOD DISHES

Listening one

List the dishes in the order they are spoken about.

Language study

Expressions to learn

- It consists of . . .
- It contains . . .
- It's made from . . .

Structures to practise

The Passive is often used to describe how things are made or done.

Look at this example:
The chef makes batter from flour, eggs and milk.
▶ *Batter **is made** from flour, eggs and milk.*

Change these sentences in the same way:
1 We make French dressing from oil and vinegar.
2 The restaurant serves lunch from 12 to 3.
3 The barman makes dry martinis from gin and vermouth.
4 The wine waiter opens the wine at the table.
5 The chef makes mornay sauce from flour, milk, butter, cheese and seasoning.
6 The waiters bring the dishes from the kitchen on trays.

New words to use

batter	garlic	new	stew
breadcrumbs	halve	poach	stuffing
breast	item	roast	take off
cover	kidney	rolled	thin
cube	melted	seasoning	tray
egg	milk	smoked	trimmings
flour			

Listening two

Listen to the descriptions of five dishes. Put these pictures in the same order and write down the ingredients in each dish.

Activity

Work in pairs. Look at the names of the ten sauces below. Only the first letter is in the correct position. Can you find out what each sauce is? When you have, talk about what the sauce consists of.

1	Aloii	6	Moshmour
2	Ograne	7	Blhceame
3	Tatoom	8	Sbuoies
4	Hselliaodna	9	Mryaon
5	Baanrisee	10	Bseegloon

Summary

Now you can
Describe dishes
Cod Mornay is cod served in cheese sauce.

Say what dishes are made from
Mornay sauce is made from butter, flour . . .

• E X T R A • W O R D S •

shellfish etc		offal
lobster	mussel	kidney
crayfish	oyster	liver
crab	scallop	tripe
prawn	squid	heart
shrimp	octopus	

14

Listening one

Listen to the tape. Then answer these questions:
1 Why are the guests complaining about their drinks order?
2 What's wrong with the steak?
3 What's wrong with the soup?
4 Why is the service slow?
5 What's wrong with the dessert?
6 What was the problem with the meat?
7 Why did the guest complain about the glass?
8 Why weren't the guests happy with their table?

Language study

Expressions to learn

■ We ordered 20 minutes ago.

■ I asked for it rare.

■ It's terribly salty.

■ I don't like to complain but . . .

■ It's quite uneatable.

■ I'm very sorry.

■ My apologies, sir.

■ I'll change it for you.

■ Can I get you something else?

■ I'll see what I can do.

Structures to practise

A The Simple Past tense is for past completed actions.

Look at these examples:
We ordered 20 minutes ago.
I asked for it rare.

Now change each verb in these sentences into the Simple Past:
1 They (arrive) at the hotel yesterday.
2 She (book) a table by phone.
3 The wine waiter (open) a bottle of Champagne.
4 The chef (cook) a wonderful meal.
5 The butter (melt) in the hot pan.
6 We (finish) our first course ten minutes ago.

For **Irregular Verbs** look at the list on page 102.

B Turn adjectives into superlatives by using . . . **est** or **most** . . .

Positive	Comparative	Superlative
bad	worse	the worst soup
slow	slower	the slowest service
draughty	draughtier	the draughtiest spot
expensive	more expensive	the most expensive dish

Put in the correct form.
Example: The service here is (quick) than in Dino's.
*The service here is **quicker** than in Dino's.*

1 The Savoy is (expensive) than the Park Hotel.
2 The service here is (slow) in town.
3 The food is (good) I've tasted.
4 The fish is (salty) than the soup.
5 Curry is our (spicy) dish.
6 Rump steak is (tough) than fillet.
7 The house wine is (popular) wine we serve.
8 We are (busy) at the weekend than during the week.

New words to use

apology	lift	taste
change	lipstick	undercooked
complain	overdone	underdone
dish	short-staffed	uneatable
draughty	spot	without
flat	stale	wonderful
immediately		

Listening two

What is the problem in each part of the dialogue?
What is the action the waiter/waitress will take?

	PROBLEM	ACTION
1		
2		
3		
4		

Activity

Which of the problems on the right can each of the things on the left sometimes have?

1	red wine	a	burnt
2	vegetables	b	overdone
3	bread	c	slow
4	milk	d	uneatable
5	meat	e	warm
6	plate	f	sour
7	service	g	dirty
8	white wine	h	flat
9	beer	i	cold
10	Coca Cola	j	undrinkable
11	coffee	k	draughty
12	champagne	l	underdone
13	table	m	stale

Summary

Now you can
Deal with customers' complaints
I'm very sorry, . . .
I'll see what I can do.

Talk about the past
I talked to the chef and . . .

Talk about the best and the worst
The most expensive restaurant in town is . . .

• E X T R A • W O R D S •

customers' complaints

tasteless	over-cooked
stringy	watery
corked	filthy
vinegary	off

15

35

Listening one

The Head Chef is showing a new Commis round the kitchen. Note down the duties of each chef and label the utensils in the picture.

CHEFS	DUTIES
Head Chef	
Assistant Chef	
Pastry Chef	

Language study

Expressions to learn

- On the premises.
- He's responsible for . . .
- This is your station.
- These are dish racks.
- Those are heat lamps.
- On the early shift.

Structures to practise

A Practise by using objects around the room:

this/these/here
This spoon
These plates
Here's the menu

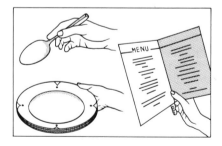

that/those/there
That spoon
Those plates
There's the menu

B Fill in the blanks with: **on, with, in, behind, for, from, into, at, to**

1 All the food is cooked . . . this kitchen.
2 Bread is baked . . . the premises.
3 The assistant chef also works . . . the line.
4 The ovens are . . . the preparation areas.
5 You start here . . . me . . . the meat and fish.
6 We prepare sauces . . . the pasta.
7 You slide the dish racks . . . the dishwasher.
8 The utensils are . . . the work stations.
9 You start . . . 7am.
10 You have a break . . . 11 . . . 12.

New words to use

assistant	flan	mincer	sharpen
baking-tin	frying-pan	oven	shift
blender	handle	pastry	sieve
bones	heat lamp	petits fours	soufflé
colander	hob	poultry	stockpot
cold store	hole	premises	supply
commis	keep	rack	utensils
croissant	kitchen	refrigerator	variety
daily	ladle	responsible	whisk
deep frier	lamp	roll	wooden
dishwasher	line	saucepan	spoon
equipment			

Listening two

Listen to the French visitor talking to a chef. Decide which name goes with each picture.

1 frying-pan   4 saucepan   6 deep frier
2 stockpot   5 soufflé dish   7 baking-tin
3 flan/tart dish

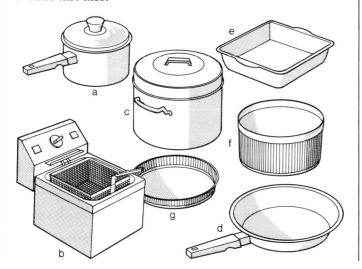

Activity

You can find all the things in the crossword below in a kitchen.

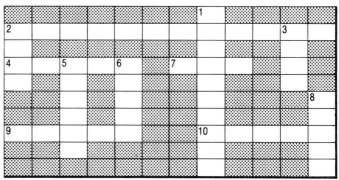

Across →

2 Food is very cold in this.
4 Heat _ _ _ _ _
7 Baking- _ _ _
9 Full of holes
10 Food from Italy

Down ↓

1 You fry food in this. (2 words)
2 Small bread loaf
3 You bake and roast in this.
5 You cut meat into very small pieces in this.
6 Hollandaise _ _ _ _ _
8 A side _ _ _ _ _

Summary

Now you can
Talk about different jobs in the kitchen
The pastry cook prepares the . . .

Identify kitchen equipment
That's a baking-tin.

Talk about kitchen equipment
The ovens are behind the preparation areas.

• E X T R A • W O R D S •

crockery

dish	side plate	teapot
bowl	cup and saucer	coffee jug
casserole	mug	hot water jug
dinner plate	egg cup	

16

Listening one

Use the information on the tape to write out the Main Course menu. The fish is turbot.

Language study

Expressions to learn

- Light the ovens.
- Get the baking tins ready.
- Julienne the carrots and celery.
- Prepare the broccoli.
- Peel and chop those apples.
- Put them through a sieve.
- Whisk up some mayonnaise.
- You mustn't do it too quickly.
- I'll see to the meat.
- What's this for?
- What's that?

Structures to practise

A Must/have to/don't have to/mustn't
Look at these sentences:

Obligation *You **must** always use fresh ingredients.*
= everybody must
*We **have to** organise the roasts.*
= it's our job

No obligation *We **don't have to** make more apple sauce.*
= it's not necessary

Prohibition *You **mustn't** smoke in the kitchen.*
= don't!

Use these forms to fill in the blanks:
1 You . . . . have clean hands in the kitchen.
2 We . . . . use fresh ingredients.
3 I . . . . be at work at 8 am.
4 You . . . . touch the switch with wet hands.
5 He . . . . work on Saturdays. He has Mondays off.
6 You . . . . work overtime this weekend, but you can if you want to.

B Why
Question: **Why** . . .? Answer: **Because** . . .

Why do we have to organize the roasts now?
Because they take a long time to cook.

What are the questions to these answers? The
cassette will help you.
1 Because then it's quicker to do them to order.
2 Because we need a purée for the apple sauce.
3 Because it curdles.

New words to use

bain-marie	dice	overtime	sauté
blanch	drained	peel	sprinkle
chop	egg yolk	prepare	strain
clarified butter	finely	purée	switch
crispy	julienne	ragout	wet
curdle	knead		

Listening two

Listen to the assistant chef giving instructions. Match
the kitchen operations with the foods she talks about.

1 mix	5 julienne	8 strain
2 knead	6 mince	9 peel
3 grill	7 whisk	10 fry
4 chop		

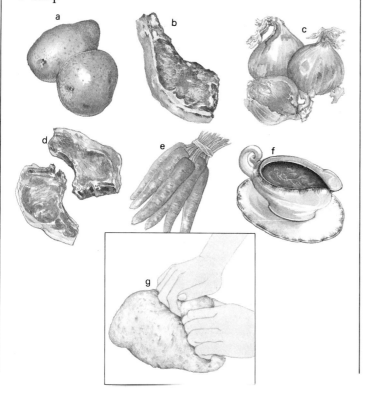

Activity

The instructions in the recipes below are not in the
right order. Work in pairs and decide what is the
correct order.

1 Mulet à la Martegale

a Sprinkle a wine glass
 of olive oil over all
b Place slices of lemon
 on top of the fish
c Wash, clean and dry
 the mullets
d Season with salt and
 pepper
e Cook in a moderate
 oven for 25–30
 minutes
f Place them in an oiled
 dish on a bed of
 tomato slices and
 onion rings

2 Sauce verte

a Add the purée to the
 mayonnaise
b Boil the herbs for 5–6
 minutes in salted water
c Prepare the
 mayonnaise
d Finish with a little
 cream
e Pass the drained herbs
 through a strainer with
 the anchovies
f Also add a little boiling
 water

Summary

Now you can
Talk about more cooking methods
You sauté the beans and I'll julienne the . . .

Give and understand instructions
First peel the potatoes.

• E X T R A • W O R D S •

kitchen equipment	other kitchen operations		
scales	baste	grease	skim
tin opener (US: can opener)	beat	blend	toss
pepper mill	glaze	score	stir-fry
chopping board	flame	parboil	
measuring jug			
peeler			

Linton Hotel
ROOM SERVICE MENU

Breakfast menu	**£4.50**
Continental breakfast	
(fruit juice, toast or croissants, tea or coffee)	
Full English Breakfast	**£7.25**
(cereals or fruit juice, fried egg, bacon,	
sausage and tomato, toast, tea or coffee)	
Hot Snacks	**£3.95**
Beefburger	
(¼ lb burger with onions and relish in bread	
roll)	**£2.60**
Toasted sandwiches	
(ham, cheese, cheese and tomato)	**£3.75**
Omelettes (aux fines herbes, mushroom)	**£1.50**
French fries (portion)	
COLD SNACKS	**£2.00**
Sandwiches	
(ham, cheese, beef, tuna fish and salad)	**£3.00**
Quiche (portion)	**£1.60**
Assorted cakes and pastries *each*	
BEVERAGES	**£ .95**
Tea per pot, per person	**£1.30**
Coffee per pot, per person	**£1.00**
Soft drinks	**£1.95**
Milk shakes (strawberry, chocolate)	**£1.20**
Hot chocolate	

Listening one

Calculate the cost of room 328's order.

Language study

Expressions to learn

- One moment, I'll put you through.
- Am I too late . . .?
- The menu is on 24 hours a day.
- Either tea or coffee.
- Anything else?

Structures to practise

Adjectives describe nouns. Adverbs describe verbs. Form adverbs by adding **-ly** to the adjective.

Adjective → adverb
A **quick** breakfast is prepared **quickly**.
A **slow** worker works **slowly**.
Fresh juice is squeezed **freshly** everyday.

Some are irregular: **good/well, hard/hard, fast/fast, late/late**

Choose the best word from the list for these sentences and fill the blank with the adverb form.

loud, quick, good, polite, hard, immediate

1 Can you serve breakfast in my room . . ., please?
2 Receptionists must speak . . . to the guests.
3 He spoke . . . into the phone as it was a bad line.
4 Items on the room service menu are prepared . . . .
5 She cooks . . . . She trained for five years.
6 They work . . . in the kitchens when the hotel is full.

New words to use

assorted	early	quiet	ticket
bacon	late	relish	toast
beefburger	loud	sandwich	trained
calculate	meeting	sausage	travel agency
cereal	milk shake	squeezed	tuna
computer	portion		

Listening two

You may have to take messages for guests. Listen to these conversations and complete the table.

	FROM	TO	MESSAGE
1			
2			
3			

Activity

Work in pairs: student A, the receptionist, with the book open giving messages; student B, Joe Williams, book closed, taking messages. Student B should repeat the message to show he understands it.

Example:
A Mr Williams, there's a message for you. Mr Longwith says he'll . . .
B Thanks! Mr Longwith says he'll . . .

Summary

Now you can
Ask guests to choose
There's orange or grapefruit juice.

Use adverbs
We have to work hard.

Offer to take phone messages
Can I give her a message?

Give someone a message
Mrs Jones called and she said she'll arrive . . .

• E X T R A • W O R D S •

hot drinks	snacks
tea (China, Indian, Russian, green, herb)	pizza
coffee (black, white)	hot dog
hot chocolate (cocoa)	croque monsieur
bouillon	toasted sandwich
mulled wine	

18

PARK HOTEL
30 Bewley Place, London W1
RESERVATIONS

Date
_____

Name of Guest   ①
_____

Date of res.   ②
_____

Room   ③   Nights   ④
_____

Contact number   ⑤
_____

Hold until   ⑥
_____

Listening one

Listen to the telephone call and fill in the card.

Language study

Expressions to learn

- We seem to have a bad line.
- Can you speak up?
- Could you spell that?
- I'm sorry, I didn't catch that.
- Did you say. . . ?
- Could you repeat that?
- Excuse me, . . . ?
- We'll hold the rooms until . . .

Structures to practise

Questions in the Simple Past use **did** + **the infinitive** of the verb.
Did you **say** . . . ? **Did** he **speak** . . . ?

Examples:
Did you say 'N'?
Yes, I said 'N'.

Did he reserve two double rooms?
Yes, he reserved two double rooms.

Make questions in the same way:
1 They arrived last night.
2 She spoke to the manager.
3 He telephoned the hotel.
4 Mr Dreyton called from Italy.
5 She ordered a dry martini.

Now say these things **didn't** happen:
Example: *They **didn't arrive** last night.*

New words to use

address	catch	letter	speak up
alphabet	country	nationality	spell
area code	hold	repeat	until

Listening two

Write down the names you hear on the tape. Can you match each name with a country?

Activity

People who come from France are French. Can you find the ten other nationalities in this word search?

```
F Q G I T A L I A N W
C B E L G I A N L P E
I N R H S I D E W S S
H T M D C G R E E K T
S C A U J T B A O D H
I S N C I K U P W Z A
T W R E X T E D Y Q M
I I A B R D A N I S H
R S L C R F F L G H M
B S P A N I S H A V S
```

Summary

Now you can
Take difficult phone calls
Could you repeat that?

Ask questions about the past
Did he arrive last night?

Spell words
F-R-A-N-C-E

Talk about countries and nationalities
Germans live in East and West Germany.

• E X T R A • W O R D S •

telephone words	countries/nationalities	
receiver	Austria	Austrian
dial	Australia	Australian
international code	Brazil	Brazilian
country code	Canada	Canadian
telephone book/directory	China	Chinese
payphone	Hungary	Hungarian
callbox	Japan	Japanese
ansaphone	Mexico	Mexican
local call	Norway	Norwegian
long distance/trunk call	Thailand	Thai
collect call	Tunisia	Tunisian
telex		
telegram		

19

Listening one

Look at the pictures. What exactly are the needs of these three guests?
Now listen to the tape. What are the needs of the guests on the tape?

Language study

Expressions to learn

My jacket needs cleaning.

I need some buttons sewn on a . . .

You needn't . . .

I don't need it until . . .

Somebody'll pick them up.

I'll send someone up.

Structures to practise

Need as a *main verb*: **need – don't need**
Need as an *auxiliary*: **need – needn't**

*The room **needs** cleaning*
*The room **doesn't need** cleaning*

*You **needn't** clean the room* (here 'clean' is the main verb)

Put the correct form of **need** into these sentences:

1 He . . . a haircut. It's very long.
2 You . . . lock the door. I'll be here.
3 They . . . a taxi. The theatre's next door.
4 He . . . a shave. He had one just now.
5 We . . . hurry. There's plenty of time.
6 She . . . a big table. She has a lot of work to do.
7 You . . . pay for the phone calls until you leave.

New words to use

available	fire	lock	same-day
blouse	foreign	next door	sew
bureau	garment	obtain	shave
button	haircut	on call	shop
cash	hairdressing	otherwise	straight
clean	hall porter	phone call	away
clothes	hire	press	theatre
currency	housekeeper	receipt	valuables
dinner-jacket	jewellery	repair	wear
facilities	laundry	safe	

Listening two

Listen to this guest asking about services. Fill in the table.

	SERVICE	WHERE	WHEN
1			
2			
3			
4			

Activity

Here is a list of hotel services. These are on the key card of the Mayfair Hotel. Match the picture with the correct heading and description. Write the name of the service next to the picture.

1 DOCTOR
2 CHEQUES
3 NIGHT PORTER
4 ROOM SERVICE
5 TRANSPORT
6 LAUNDRY
7 SHOE CLEANING
8 VALUABLES
9 THEATRE TICKETS
10 CAR PARKING
11 TEA AND COFFEE

12 These can be obtained by . . .
13 The Cashier will . . .
14 Please deposit your . . .
15 A same-day service . . .
16 In an emergency, . . .
17 Snacks, drinks and . . .
18 There are facilities for . . .
19 The hotel has car . . .
20 From 10 pm the . . .
21 For car hire, . . .
22 Shoes should be . . .

Summary

Now you can
Deal with guests' requests for service
I'll send some up for you.

Explain how a service operates
I'll give you a receipt and put them in the safe.

• E X T R A • W O R D S •

clothes	hotel activities (other)	
shirt	excursions	aerobics
dress	barbeque	cabaret/floor show
skirt	keep fit	folk evenings
suit		

Welcome to the
MAYFAIR HOTEL

a _____
b _____
c _____
d _____
e _____
f _____
g _____
h _____
i _____
j _____
k _____
l _____
m _____
n _____
o _____
p _____
q _____
r _____
s _____
t _____
u _____
v _____

FIRE INSTRUCTIONS
Please read the Fire Notice on display
in your room.

20

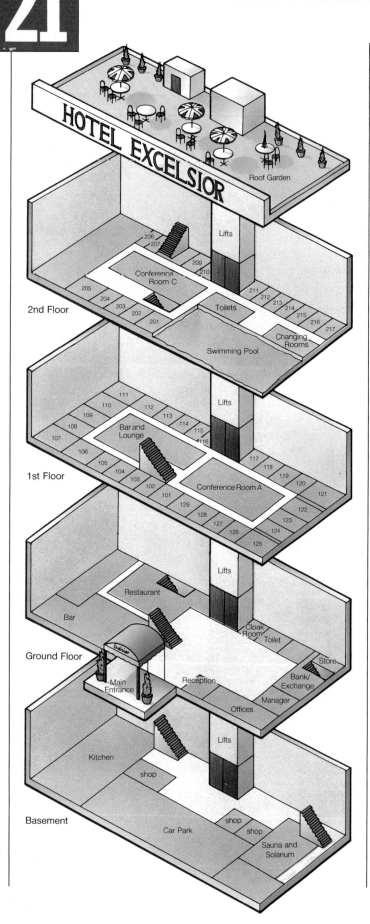

Listen to the directions and mark the 5 places on the plan:

Language study

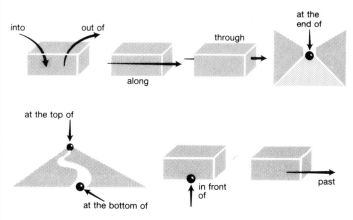

Expressions to learn

It's on the first/second/ground floor.

Take the lift to . . .

Turn left/right.

Walk along/Go down the corridor.

Go through the doorway.

Go past the . . .

Go across the lobby.

It's at the end/top/bottom of the . . .

When you come out of the lift, . . .

. . . on the other side.

Structures to practise

Study the diagrams and check with your teacher that you have understood the exact meaning of the prepositions.

Using the plan of the hotel, write or working in pairs give directions from reception to:

1 the swimming pool
2 the sauna
3 room 158
4 the exchange bureau
5 the Manager's office
6 the car park
7 the bar

New words to use

air-conditioning	dressing-table	opposite
armchair	facing	outdoor
basement	flower shop	roof garden
bath	foyer	shaver point
beauty salon	fridge	shelf
bedside table	gift shop	shower
blind	golf-course	socket
bottom	ground floor	stairs
chest of drawers	gymnasium (gym)	stamp
conference	hanger	stool
corridor	horse-riding	television
curtain	indoor	upstairs
downstairs	lobby	wardrobe

Listening two

Listen to the Housekeeper talking to a new member of staff. Label the picture.

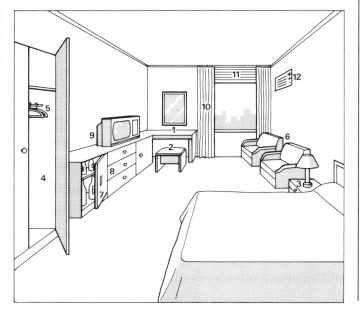

Activity

Look at the three hotels below. Which of the list of facilities should each of them have?

1 travel agency
2 golf-course
3 car park
4 laundry
5 outdoor swimming-pool
6 beauty salon
7 tennis courts
8 car-hire office
9 night porter
10 exchange bureau
11 flower shop
12 horse-riding
13 hairdressing salon
14 indoor swimming-pool
15 gymnasium (gym)

Summary

Now you can
Explain how to get to different parts of the hotel
Go downstairs, turn left at the . . .

Talk about the contents of guests' rooms
The bedroom contains a bed, dressing table, . . .

• E X T R A • W O R D S •

bathroom		more activities
towels	bidet	ice-skating
soap	bath mat	skiing
shower cap	shampoo	hiking
taps		bicycle hire
wash basin		bowling

21

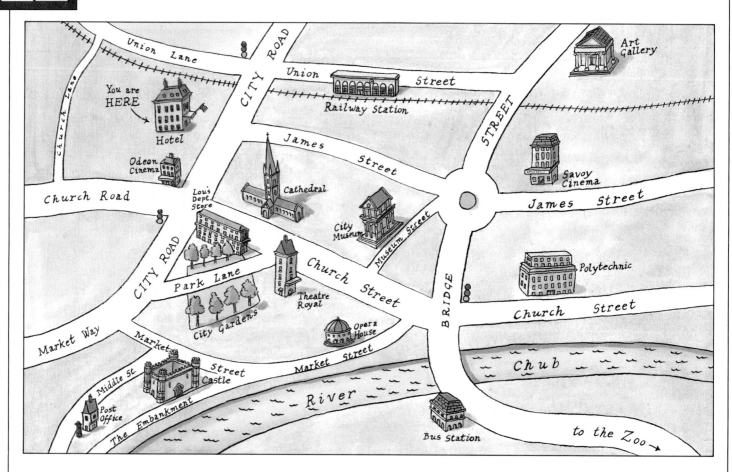

Listening one

As you listen, follow the guests' routes on the map. What places of interest do they pass?

Language study

Expressions to learn

▨ Is it far?

▨ No, not far.

▨ About ten minutes' walk/on foot.

▨ Turn left outside . . .

▨ Go down to the traffic lights.

▨ Go straight on at the crossroads.

▨ Carry on down . . .

▨ . . . along on your right.

Structures to practise

Prepositions are easy to use once you understand their sense. There are a few exceptions. Note that we say 'on foot' but 'by car', 'by bus'.

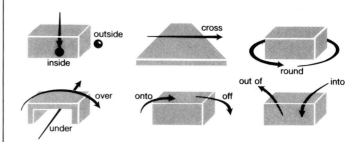

Where are you going? Put the correct prepositions below and see where you get to:

When you leave the hotel, turn right and go (1) . . . City Road. Turn left (2) . . . the traffic lights (3) . . . Church Street. Go (4) . . . Lou's and the Theatre Royal and take the next right turn. Along (5) . . . your right you'll see the (6) . . . .

New words to use

art gallery	direct	on foot	show
bridge	far	opera	straight ahead
bus	further	outside	subway
castle	inside	post office	T junction
cathedral	map	railway	traffic lights
cinema	museum	round	train
department store	near	roundabout	zoo

Listening two

Look at the map of the London Underground. You will hear descriptions of how to get to three places of interest in London from different starting points: Euston, St Paul's, and Liverpool Street. Make a note of the route, final station and destination.

Activity

Work in pairs. Use the hotel plan in Unit 21 and the town and London Underground maps in this unit to ask for and give directions.

Summary

Now you can

Give directions around the city
Go down the street and over the bridge.

Give directions about public transport
Get on at Piccadilly and change at. . .

Identify places of interest
The cathedral is opposite Lou's Department Store.

• E X T R A • W O R D S •

transport	street terms	road signs
by car	dead end/cul de sac	Stop
by bus	pavement/sidewalk	Give Way
by train	footpath	One Way
by plane	no through road	No Entry
by air	pedestrian street/footstreet	No Parking
on foot	main road	

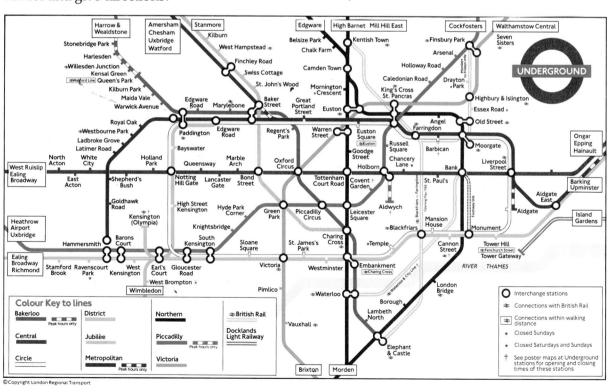

© Copyright London Regional Transport

22

23

Listening one

Listen to the tape, then answer the comprehension questions.

Comprehension check

1 What has Mrs Johnson planned for today?
2 What is on at the art gallery?
3 What does the hall porter advise her to see?
4 What has happened on the steps outside the hotel?
5 What does the hall porter offer to do?
6 Why does he suggest calling an ambulance?
7 What does he ask Jim to do?

Language study

Expressions to learn

What have you planned?

Have you heard anything about the . . . ?

You ought to go to the . . .

I believe it's . . .

They have some . . .

I'll send the porter right away.

I'll phone the . . .

I think you should have . . .

OFFERING HELP AND ADVICE

Structures to practise

A We saw in Unit 15 that the Simple Past tense is used for past completed actions:
We ordered 20 minutes ago.

The Present Perfect tense is used for actions which have not yet finished:
We haven't ordered yet.
Or for actions which have recently finished:
We have just ordered.

Complete these pairs of sentences by putting the verb into the correct tense:
1 (visit, you) the new exhibition yet?
  Yes, I (go) last night.
2 We (see) the show at the theatre last Sunday.
  Is it good? I (not, see) it yet.
3 (arrive, Mr Tonini) yet?
  Yes, he (register) an hour ago.
4 (finish, you) the exercise?
  Yes, we (finish, just).

B Look at these two sentences:

*Mr Lascelles' leg **may/might** be broken.* (might = less certain)
*They **ought to/should** call an ambulance.* (same meaning)

Match these pairs of sentences:
1 It may rain   a. You should call a doctor
2 It may be serious   b. You should go this week
3 They might phone   c. You ought to take an
4 He may arrive late   umbrella
5 The play finishes   d. You ought to leave a
  on Saturday   message
                 e. We should hold the
                 room until 10 pm

New words to use

ambulance	emergency	modern	time of year
believe	exhibit	painkiller	umbrella
break	exhibition	permanent	visit
Casualty	fall	plan	well
chemists	garage	prescription	wound
comfortable	glasses	serious	X-ray
dizzy	health	shoemaker	
dressing	leg	strap	

Listening two

Listen to three guests with problems. Write, for each guest, what the problem is and the remedy (ies) suggested.

Activity

Work in pairs, one as a guest with a problem, the other as a receptionist offering help and advice.

a. a stomach ache   b. a missing car   c. broken glasses   d. a stolen handbag   e. a cut finger
f. a broken sandal strap   g. a headache
h. a broken down car   i. a toothache

Summary

Now you can
Talk to guests about their day
What have you planned today?

Give advice
You ought to call a doctor.

Help guests with their problems
I'll phone a . . . for you.

• EXTRA • WORDS •

health problems	emergency services	health care personnel
a cold	ambulance service	doctor
influenza (flu)	fire brigade	nurse
headache	police	dentist
stomach ache		optician
diarrhoea		
toothache		

24

Listening one

As you listen, fill in the gaps in the complaints.

1 My room . . . . hasn't been . . . . since the last guest.
The carpet's . . . . , the bed's . . . . and the
bathroom . . . . touched.

2 Our room isn't ready for us. . . . . no
towels, ... , or toilet paper in the . . . . .

3 Can you do something about the . . . . in my room?
It's only running . . . . And the . . . . in my
bedside lamp . . . . work.

4 The . . . . in 302 next door is . . . . . I . . . . sleep.

Language study

Expressions to learn

My room hasn't been cleaned.

The noise is awful.

The bathroom hasn't been touched.

It should've been done.

I'll send someone up.

I'll speak to . . .

Structures to practise

A It may not be your job to help guests personally
with their needs, but you can organise things that
should have been done for them.

Look at these sentences:
My room hasn't been cleaned.
*The maids **should've cleaned it**.* or
*It **should've been cleaned**.*

Now answer other complaints in the same way:

1 The sheets haven't been changed.
2 The TV hasn't been fixed.
3 The shower hasn't been repaired.
4 My shoes haven't been cleaned.
5 My wine hasn't been opened.
6 My luggage hasn't been brought in.

B After saying that something **should've been done**, you need to tell the guest that you **will** deal with the problem.

Example:
Our room hasn't been cleaned.
It **should've been cleaned. I'll contact** Housekeeping *straight away*.

Now answer these complaints in the same way:
1 The waste-paper basket hasn't been emptied.
2 The carpet is dirty.
3 The soap and towels haven't been replaced.
4 My laundry hasn't been returned.
5 The shower isn't working.

New words to use

awful	obviously	sugar
bowl	replace	toilet paper
bulb/light bulb	running	touch
carpet	see to	towel
check in	sheet	unmade
maid	sleep	waste-paper basket
noise	soap	

Listening two

Listen to this biography of a famous chef and then fill in the missing information below.

George Auguste
1 . . . . . born 1846

⬇

First job 2 . . . . . .

⬇

1865 moved to
3 . . . . . .

⬇

In 4 . . . . . Monte Carlo
5 . . . . . Hotel

⬇

1890 went to 6 . . . . . .
to manage 7 . . . . . .

⬇

With Ritz he opened Hotel
Ritz in 8 . . . . . . and
9 . . . . . Hotel in London

⬇

1903 'Le Guide Culinaire'

⬇

1919 returned to
10 . . . . . .

Activity

Work in pairs, one as a guest complaining about the state of the room, the other as the receptionist promising to put things right.

Summary

Now you can
Understand complaints
The sheets haven't been changed.

Deal with complaints
I'm sorry, I'll send someone up straight away.

• E X T R A • W O R D S •

stationery	room equipment	bed equipment
writing paper	mirror	bedspread
envelopes	door	blanket
note pad	alarm clock	pillow
telex form	radio	pillowcase
fax form	video facility	mattress
post cards	sewing kit	duvet
	Do Not Disturb sign	

24

25

St. James Hotel				
BILL RECORD CARD				
Bill No.	692	Name of guest		Adams
Cash		Service incl.		
Credit card		VAT		
Cheque		receipt		
Bankers card		cashier		PMS

Listening one

Listen to the tape and tick the tables with details of each bill.

Fratelli's of Liverpool				
BILL RECORD		**NUMBER:** 530		
Cash		Tip		
Credit card		Receipt		
Cheque				
Bankers card		Cashier		RMH

Language study

Expressions to learn

- How are you paying?
- Service and tax are included.
- Would you sign here, please?
- Your signature here, please.
- Here's your receipt.
- Do you have a banker's card?
- Do you have some form of identification?
- Don't worry, sir. I'll stamp it.

Structures to practise

A The Present Continuous tense is used for actions which are happening now.

Look at these sentences:

How are you paying?	**now**
How do you pay?	**usually**
How did you pay?	**last time**

Answer these questions about **now.**
1 What are you doing?
2 Where are you sitting?
3 What book are you using?
4 What are you studying?
5 What's your teacher doing?

B Look at these pairs of sentences:

Your bill's ready.
*I'll settle **it** now.*

Where are the telephone calls?
*I put **them** at the top.*

Who shall I make a cheque out to?
*I'll stamp **it** for you.*

Object pronouns

singular	plural
me	us
you	you
him	
her	them
it	

Put the correct Object pronoun in each blank:
1 Where's your key?
   I gave . . . to the porter.
2 Where did you put the sheets?
   I put . . . in room 201.
3 Did you tell Mrs Dupont her husband called?
   Yes, I gave . . . the message.
4 Where's Jim?
   I saw . . . a moment ago.
5 I'm glad you and your family enjoyed your stay.
   You looked after . . . very well.
6 Goodbye.
   Goodbye, we hope to see . . . again.

New words to use

amount	identification	signature
banker's card	include	stamp
check out	pay	total
cheque	settle	traveller's cheque
credit card	sign	Value Added Tax (VAT)

Listening two

What nationality is each of these customers and how did they pay their bills?

Activity

Find the ten currencies in this word search:

O	N	F	D	O	L	L	A	R	P
L	P	E	A	S	I	M	Y	W	E
Z	O	G	Y	F	R	A	N	C	S
G	U	I	L	D	E	R	S	R	E
A	N	Y	J	R	S	K	C	O	T
H	D	V	X	U	D	S	R	W	A
E	S	C	U	D	O	S	E	N	S

Summary

Now you can
Take payment of bills
How are you paying, sir?

See to the necessary administration for payment
Can you sign here, please?

Use object pronouns
*I gave **him** the message yesterday.*

• E X T R A • W O R D S •

currencies	payment	
Lire	total	account
Escudos	exchange rate	charge
Swiss francs	room rate	discount
Drachma	tariff	supplement
Guilders	tax	
Belgian francs		

25

26

Listening one

Now listen to two other guests querying their bills.
Then answer the comprehension questions.

Comprehension check

1 Why does the guest query the telephone calls on the bill?
2 What is the cost of calling from the hotel?
3 How many units did she use?
4 What's the second query?
5 Whose mistake is it?
6 How does the diner want to pay his bill?
7 What are his queries?
8 What is the mistake?

Language study

Expressions to learn

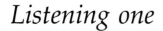 It can't be right.

I'll check it for you.

I'm afraid there's no mistake.

I beg your pardon, that's our mistake.

I'm sorry about that.

Structures to practise

When talking about quantity, use **a lot of** with affirmative verbs:

There is	**a lot of**	rooms guests chairs
There are		money beer information

Use **much** with negative verbs and questions about uncountable nouns:

There isn't	**much**	money beer information
Is there(?)		

Use **many** with negative verbs and questions about countable nouns:

There aren't	**many**	rooms guests chairs
Are there(?)		

Fill in the blanks with **a lot of**, **much** or **many**:
1 There aren't . . . people in tonight.
2 There's . . . preparation to do.
3 Do you have . . . single rooms?
4 There isn't . . . time before we open.
5 There are . . . vegetables to prepare.
6 Do we have . . . hot starters today?
7 Is there . . . work to do this morning?
8 There are . . . beds to make.

New words to use

accept	confused	layout	rate
balance	corner	mistake	salmon
cashier	deposit	package tour	unit
company	diner	query	

Listening two

The Head Cashier is showing a new cashier the layout of a computer bill. As you listen, fill in the details.

MOUNT ROYAL HOTEL NEWCASTLE

① [   ]   SUNSHINE REF: S22339/1

DEPOSIT: ② [   ]

Room ③ [   ]   No of guests ⑤ [   ]   Arrive 17/03/88

Rate ④ [   ]   Bill no 2601 283 W M 2   Depart 19/03/88

	CHARGES	CREDITS	BALANCE
17.03.88 Apartments	60		233992
18.03.88 Apartments	60		
19.03.88 Ledger			
Transfer	[ ] ⑥	S22339/1 ⑦ [ ]	

ACC. TO: SUNSHINE HOLIDAYS

Service/Goods	£	
Value Added Tax	% £	
	Sub-total £	
Non-Taxable Items	£	
	GRAND TOTAL £	

SIGNATURE _____

SERVICE AND TAX ARE
INCLUDED, GRATUITIES AT   **PLEASE LEAVE YOUR KEY**
YOUR DISCRETION

Activity

Put these countries, nationalities or currencies into the correct column below. Then complete the table.

Yen	Lira	France	Guilder
British	Peseta	Spain	Portuguese
Belgian	USA	Escudo	

COUNTRY	NATIONALITY	CURRENCY

Summary

Now you can
Clarify payment queries
I'll just check for you.

Apologize for mistakes
I'm sorry about that.

Recognize the currencies of different countries
dollars, Deutschmarks, pounds

• E X T R A • W O R D S •

bills		**service**
invoice	debit	service charge
voucher	credit	gratuity
coupon	deposit	tip
sub-total	amount	
balance		

26

Listening one

Listen to the cassette and fill in the blanks in the conversations.

Language study

Expressions to learn

- I hope you enjoyed your stay.
- We did very much thank you.
- We're flying to . . . today.
- We're going to see . . .
- This looks like your taxi.
- I hope we'll see you again.
- Have a pleasant trip.
- Safe journey.

Structures to practise

Several tenses are used when talking about the future.
These 5 sentences are all about the future.

It **leaves** at midnight.	times
We**'re flying** to Florida tonight.	plans or arrangements
We**'re going** to see our daughter.	future intentions
I hope we**'ll see** you again. If we're in Lyon again we**'ll stay** here.	forecasting

Answer these questions about your future using:
I'm going to . . . or **I'll . . .**

1 What'll you do when you finish at college?
2 What sort of job do you hope to get?
3 Where will you live?
4 Where will you live if the job is far away?
5 How will you spend your first month's salary?
6 Are you going to travel to other countries?
7 Where do you hope to go?

New words to use

briefcase	fly	looks like	spend
college	forget	lost	stay
daughter	hope	money	trip
departure	job	pleasant	underground
family	journey	salary	waste

Listening two

Listen to these three guests leaving. Write in the table if they are leaving a hotel or a restaurant, where they are going and how they are getting there.

	HOTEL/ RESTAURANT	DESTINATION	TRANSPORT
1			
2			
3			

Activity

In pairs, A and B, use the page from B's diary and the example dialogue to fix an evening at the cinema. Then make a diary for next week. You are busy on five nights. With your partner make dialogues to find a free evening.

Example: A. What are you doing on Tuesday evening? Can you come to the cinema?
B. No I'm going to Tom's.   etc.

Summary

Now you can
Say goodbye to guests
Goodbye. Have a good trip. Safe journey.

See to their needs as they leave
Shall I ask a porter . . .

Talk about future plans and intentions
When I get home I'm going to write a letter.

• E X T R A • W O R D S •

family

mother	uncle	brother
father	nephew	sister
son	niece	step-brother
father-in-law	grandfather	half-sister
daughter-in-law	grandmother	guardian
aunt	cousin	

27

GRAND EUROPOLITAN HOTELS
Personnel Department
INTERVIEW RECORD CARD
_____

Surname: ① _____

First names: ② _____

Address: ③ _____

_____

Job applied for: ④ _____

Qualifications: ⑤ _____

Experience: ⑥ _____

_____

Previous employers: ⑦ _____

_____

_____

Available from: ⑧ _____

Listening one

As you listen, fill in the form.

Language study

Expressions to learn

▥ Dear Sir/Madam . . .

▥ Yours faithfully . . .

▥ Dear Mr/Mrs/Miss/Ms. . . .

▥ Yours sincerely . . .

▥ I would like to enquire . . .

▥ With reference to . . .

▥ Would you please send me . . .

▥ I enclose an s.a.e. (stamped addressed envelope) . . .

Structures to practise

For business letters, polite formality is required. Do not use short forms of verbs.

Use the information in the interview and the language in the Expressions to complete these letters.

Dear Sir/ ① . . . . . .,
Re vacancy for receptionist
② . . . . . . to apply for the job of receptionist which you advertised in this month's 'Hotel Employ'.
③ . . . . . . send me an application form. I ④ . . . . . . an s.a.e.

Yours ⑤ . . . . . .

⑥ . . . . . . *Martine Nouveau*

Dear Miss Nouveau,
      Re vacancy for ⑦ . . . . . .
⑧ . . . . . . for your letter. We are not sending ⑨ . . . . . . for this job.
You are invited for interview at the above ⑩ . . . . . . on Friday April 3 1988. Interviews will be between 9 am and 11.30 am.

⑪ . . . . . . sincerely,

Jeanne Deveau

Personnel Department

New words to use

advertise	enclose	marital status
advertisement	enquire	married
applicant	experience	notice
application form	high-class	part-time
copy	interview	previous
education	invite	surname
employer	mainly	vacancy

Listening two

Listen to the cassette and then answer these job advertisements for the speaker in writing.

COMMIS CHEF

Our Egon Ronay recommended kitchen requires a person who is college trained. Live in/out. Good conditions.
Application forms from:
The Head Chef
Spread Eagle Hotel,
17 Park Town,
Oxford OX4 1QD

Tel: (0865) 58157

COMMIS CHEF

To assist our young Head Chef. This is a small internationally known, 14-bedroom hotel with a 40-seater restaurant and busy lunchtime buffet, high standards of English/Continental cuisine. Single accommodation provided.
Apply in writing with full C.V. and references to:
The Proprietor, Avon Bridge Hotel
Bath Street, Glastonbury, Somerset
Tel: (0458) 726106

Activity

The following crossword has mainly job application words:

Across →

1. You know how to answer an _____.
5. I live at this _____.
7. I enclose a copy of my __.
8. I am _____ from the beginning of July.
9. Another word for salary.
10. He has a lot of _____. He has worked in six hotels.
12. Date of _____.

Down ↓

1. Father or mother's sister.
2. Hotel Bristol has a _____ for a part-time cashier.
3. You are invited for _____ on 5 June at 10 am.
4. Give your full ____.
6. I am going to _____ for the job at the Golden Fork.
11. We are ___ sending application forms for this job.

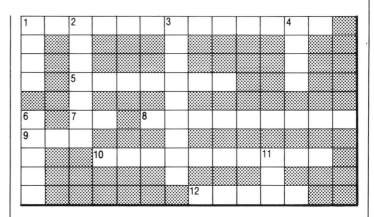

Summary

Now you can
Take part in a job interview
Lay out a short business letter
Fill in an application form
Answer an advertisement

• EXTRA • WORDS •

personal details

single
married
widow
CV (curriculum vitae)
biodata
training

letter abbreviations

s.a.e.
re
a.s.a.p.
i.e.
e.g.

28

Unit 1

Listening one

1
Reception: Good morning, Park Hotel. Can I help you?
Caller: I'd like to book a single room for three nights.
Recep: Yes, madam. Could I have your name, please?
Caller: Mrs Andrews.

2
Waitress: Good afternoon, Garden Restaurant. Can I help you?
Caller: I'd like to reserve a table for six, for Wednesday evening.
Waitress: Yes, what name, please?
Caller: My name's Jackson.

3
Waiter: Good evening, Fratelli's.
Caller: Could I speak to the Manager, please?
Waiter: Yes, who's calling?
Caller: Mr Evans.

4
Reception: Good morning, Carlton Hotel. Can I help you?
Caller: Hello, can I have Reservations, please?
Recep: One moment, please.

Listening two

Reception: Good evening, sir. Can I help you?
Guest: Yes, I phoned on Saturday to book a room.
Recep: What name is it?
Guest: Branston.
Recep: Ah yes, Mr Branston, a single room. Number 407, for two nights.
Guest: Oh, and I'd like to reserve a table for dinner.
Recep: Yes, sir. I'll give your reservation to the restaurant. What time . . .

Unit 2

Listening one

1
Mr Hopkins: Hello, I'm George Hopkins. Can you tell me a little about the hotel?
Reception: Yes, I'd be glad to. The hotel's in the centre of the city. There's a restaurant and a coffee shop, and there are two bars. The cost is £55 for a single room. What else can I tell you? Oh yes, there's a sauna and a swimming-pool.

2
Woman: Could you tell me about Fratelli's bar and restaurant?
Head Waiter: The restaurant is at 16 Side Street. There's an à la carte menu at lunchtime and in the evening. At lunchtime there's also a special three course table d'hôte menu. The price per person is £11.50.

Listening two

1
Reception: The charge for the single room is 850 francs per night.
Guest: That includes breakfast, I hope?
Recep: It does, sir, yes.

2
Guest: Is there a children's menu?
Waiter: Yes, sir, there's a special children's menu at £5.

3
Guest: A small beer, please.
Barman: There you are, sir. That's 1 dollar 25.

4
Guest: How much is the double room?
Reception: It's £65 per night, including breakfast.

5
Guest: Is the table d'hôte menu still £14?
Waiter: No, I'm sorry, it's now £16.50.

Dialogues

Unit 3

Listening one

Head Waiter: Dino's, can I help you?
Woman: Can I speak to the Head Waiter, please?
Head W: Speaking. How can I help you?
Woman: I'd like to book a table. What time do you serve lunch?
Head W: We serve lunch from 12.00 to 2.30.
Woman: OK . . . are you open every day?
Head W: From Tuesday to Sunday. We're closed on Mondays in winter.
Woman: Can I book a table for Sunday, please?
Head W: Certainly, madam. How many for?
Woman: For 6 people.
Head W: And what time?
Woman: For one o'clock.
Head W: What name is it, please?
Woman: My name is Mrs Richards.
Head W: Table for 6 on Sunday at 1 pm. Thank you very much, Mrs Richards. Goodbye.
Woman: Goodbye.

Listening two

It's nine o'clock.
It's a quarter past two.
It's twenty to eight.
It's half past one.
It's a quarter to six.
It's twenty past eleven.

We can also say:
It's nine.
It's two fifteen.
It's seven forty.
It's one thirty.
It's five forty-five.
It's eleven twenty.

1 We're having breakfast at a quarter to eight.
2 When does your plane leave? At ten o'clock, I think.
3 OK, I'll see you this evening at six forty-five.
4 I'm meeting him at five past two.
5 Lunch is at half past twelve.
6 The film begins at eight twenty-five.

Unit 4

Listening one

1
Can I book a double room for tonight?
I'm sorry, we're fully booked for tonight.

2
Could I reserve a table for two for tonight?
I'm afraid we haven't any tables left for tonight.

3
Can I reserve a table for Sunday lunch?
I'm very sorry. We don't open on Sundays.

4
Could I book a family room for the Christmas weekend?
I'm afraid we haven't any rooms left that weekend.

5
Can I reserve a table for tomorrow night?
I'm sorry, sir, we've nothing left. It's our busy night.

6
Can I speak to Mr Yossarian in room 101?
I'm sorry, there's no answer. Can I take a message?

Listening two

. . . the room costs 70 dollars . . . He's coming on Wednesday . . . at 2.15, I think . . . the menu at 90 francs? . . . OK, Tuesday, at 5.25 . . . the children's menu is 18 marks . . . see you on Saturday morning then . . . £60, that's a lot for a room . . . the bar is open at half past ten . . .

Unit 5

Listening one

1
Reception: Good evening, can I help you?
Guest: Yes, I'd like a room for two nights.
Recep: Do you have a reservation?
Guest: Yes, the name's Bray. I telephoned you on April 2nd.
Recep: Ah yes, Mr Bray. Could you fill in this registration card, please?
Guest: Is it necessary to fill in the passport information?
Recep: Yes, if you would, please. Here's your key. It's room number 86 on the third floor. And here's your key card for use in the hotel's bars and restaurants. I'll ask the porter to help you with your luggage . . .

2
Maître d'hôtel: Good evening.
Guest: A table for three, please.
M.d': Do you have a reservation?
Guest: Yes.
M.d': What name, please?
Guest: Gibson.
M.d': Come this way, please, and I'll show you to your table.
Guest: Thank you.
M.d': Can I take your coats first . . .

Listening two

1 What date is the second Monday?
2 What day is the sixteenth?
3 What date is the last Friday?
4 Is the fourth a Friday?
5 What day is the tenth?
6 What date is the first Thursday?
7 Is the thirteenth a Wednesday?
8 What date is the first Tuesday?
9 What is the last day of the month?

Unit 6

Listening one

Barman: Good evening, sir. What can I get you?
Tim: A pint of beer, please. What would you like, Denise?
Denise: A gin and tonic, please.
Barman: Would you like ice and lemon in that, madam?
Denise: Yes, please.
Tim: Ah, here's Michael. What'll you have, Mike?
Michael: Oh, a dry sherry for Jill, and a lager for me, Tim.
Barman: Would you like a pint or a half, sir?
Tim: Make it a pint.
Barman: Thank you, sir. Shall I charge this to your room?
Tim: Yes, please.
Barman: May I have your key card please, sir?
Tim: Oh yes, here you are.

Listening two

1
Barman: Good evening, sir. What can I get you?
Customer: A large whisky for me, please, and a large gin and tonic for my wife.

2
Customer: Oh, barman, could I have a half of cider and a small rum, please?
Barman: Certainly, sir.

3
Barman: Can I help you, madam?
Customer: Yes, I'd like a small vodka and tonic, and a double rum and lemonade.
Barman: Would you like ice in both, madam?

4
Customer: Two pints of lager, please, and two single whiskies.
Barman: Yes, sir.

5
Customer: Two lemonades, two halves of bitter, a cider, and a double gin and tonic, please.

Unit 7

Listening one

Trainee: How do you mix a dry martini?
Steward: First check you have everything you need. Then take a glass, polish it, and fill it with ice.
T: Which shape glass?
S: A special dry martini glass.
T: OK, what next?
S: Next take a large glass and quarter fill it with ice.
T: Mm.
S: Then add two measures of London dry gin.
T: OK.
S: And then pour in a small measure of dry vermouth, just a dash.
T: I see.
S: Finally, give it a good stir with a bar spoon to mix and chill the liquids.
T: Is that all?
S: No, throw out the ice from the glass, and then strain the dry martini into the glass.
T: Do you decorate it?
S: Yes, but not with slices of lemon or parasols. You always have an olive on a cocktail stick.

Listening two

OK, this morning I'm going to tell you about two cocktails, the Daiquiri and the Manhattan.
Let's start with the Daiquiri. First take the cocktail shaker and half fill it with broken ice. Then add five centilitres of lime juice. After that put in four centilitres of rum and one or two dashes of grenadine. Then shake it well and pass it through a strainer into a cocktail glass. All right? Are there any questions . . .

Let's move on to the next cocktail, the Manhattan. No shaker for this one, just a large glass. Half fill this glass with ice and add four centilitres of Canadian Club whisky, then four centilitres of Italian vermouth, and one or two dashes of Angostura bitters. Stir it well, then pass it through a strainer into a cocktail glass. Serve it with a cherry.

Unit 8

Listening one

Waiter: Good evening, madam, evening, sir. Can I take your coats?
Guests: Thank you.
Waiter: Here are the menus and the wine list. Would you like to order an aperitif?
Man: Yes, I'll have a Campari and soda. What about you, dear?
Woman: A medium dry sherry, please.
Waiter: Thank you.

Waiter: Here we are. One medium dry sherry and a Campari and soda. Are you ready to order now?
Man: Yes, I think so.
Waiter: What would you like to start with?
Woman: What's the soup of the day?
Waiter: Cream of mushroom.
Man: I'll have the mixed hors d'œuvres, please.
Woman: The melon and Parma ham for me, please.
Waiter: One mixed hors d'œuvres and one melon and Parma ham, thank you.
Man: Oh, and can we have some bread, please?

Listening two

1
Man: Grilled sardines for me. What about you, Jean?
Woman: I'll have the avocado pear.
Waiter: Right, so that's one grilled sardines and one avocado pear with prawns.
Man: Yes . . .

2
Waiter: Would you like to order now?
Woman: Yes, we'd like two melon with Parma ham, please.
Waiter: Yes, madam.
Woman: Oh and a bottle of still mineral water.
Waiter: Certainly.

3
Man: Can you tell me what the soup of the day is?
Waiter: Yes, it's cream of mushroom soup.
Man: Oh . . . I think I'll have the pâté, then. And after that I'd like a . . .

4
Woman: The melon with Parma ham for me, please.
Waiter: I'm sorry, madam, there's no more melon.
Woman: OK, I'll have the mixed hors d'œuvres instead.

5 8

Unit 9

Listening one

Waiter: What would you like to follow?

Man: What's this?

Waiter: It's a Greek dish – a kind of pie with layers of aubergine and lamb and tomatoes, topped with a creamy cheese sauce.

Woman: I think I'll have some fish, please.

Waiter: I'm afraid we haven't any sole left, madam, but the turbot is excellent.

Woman: Then I'll have the turbot.

Man: I think I'll settle for a steak.

Waiter: Rump or fillet, sir?

Man: Rump, please.

Waiter: And how would you like it cooked?

Man: Medium rare.

Waiter: What vegetables would you like with your fish, madam?

Woman: The duchesse potatoes, please, and some spinach.

Waiter: And you sir?

Man: Oh, jacket potato, mushrooms, and a side salad, please.

Waiter: Thank you.

Listening two

Waiter: . . . and for the main courses they'd like . . .

Sous-chef: That's table 17 you mean?

Waiter: yeah . . . one scampi and one duckling.

S-chef: Any vegetables?

Waiter: Yes, spinach, green beans, and a side salad.

S-chef: Fine, any others?

Waiter: Yes, table 6. A fillet steak, rare, french fries and a side salad.

S-chef: OK.

Waiter: Table 11, John.

S-chef: OK.

Waiter: A veal escalope, a turbot, one green beans and a jacket potato.

S-chef: Right you are.

Unit 10

Listening one

Wine Waiter: Good evening, sir, madam. Would you like something to drink with your meal?

Man: Yes, please. We'd like half a bottle of dry white wine. Which is drier, the Chablis or the Liebfraumilch?

Wine W: The German wine is sweeter than the French one, but the Chablis is not as dry as the Muscadet.

Woman: Let's have the Chablis then, please.

Man: OK, and a bottle of red please. Is the Beaujolais as full-bodied as the Beaune?

Wine W: Not quite, sir. The Beaujolais is lighter than the Beaune. These Bordeaux wines are full-bodied.

Man: OK, a bottle of the Bergerac then, please.

Wine W: Thank you, sir. Would you like some mineral water?

Woman: Some still mineral water, please.

Wine W: Certainly, madam.

Listening two

In Portugal, Oporto is the centre of the wine area. Dāo is the name of the district south of Oporto and port wine comes from the area north of the town. In Spain, the most famous wine, sherry, comes from the extreme south. But there are lighter Spanish wines, too. The best of these lighter table wines come from Rioja, north of Madrid. In France, the Champagne district produces the most famous sparkling wine. That's east of Paris. South of Paris, and running west to Nantes, is the Loire Valley which produces wines like Muscadet and Sancerre. The Bordeaux region is in the south-west of France. This area produces Médoc, St Emilion, and Graves, for example. Just north of Lyon is the Burgundy wine district, the home of Beaujolais, Mâcon, and many others. In Italy, the most famous wine, Chianti, comes from the area south of Florence. The district to the east of Rome produces a famous white wine, Frascati.

Unit 11

Listening one

Woman: That was lovely.
Waiter: Good. I'm glad you enjoyed it. Would you like a sweet?
Man: Mm. what've you got?
Waiter: One moment, sir, I'll bring the dessert trolley. . . . Here we are.
Woman: Can you tell us what they are?
Waiter: On the top there's apple pie, chocolate gâteau, Charlotte Russe or fresh fruit salad, and underneath there's profiteroles, blackcurrant cheese-cake and, of course, the fresh fruit basket.
Man: What about cheese?
Waiter: On the cheese board we have English Cheddar, Stilton, Camembert, and Dolce Latte.
Man: Are you having cheese, Jill?
Woman: No, just a dessert for me, the chocolate gâteau, I think.
Waiter: Would you like cream, madam?
Woman: No, thank you.
Man: And I'll have a piece of Stilton with biscuits, and then some fruit salad.
Waiter: Cream, sir?
Man: Please, and we'd like coffee to follow.
Waiter: Certainly, sir. Would you like a liqueur with your coffee?
Man: What about you, Jill? . . . No, thanks.

Listening two

There are three main types of cheese in Europe. The first of these is the hard type. There are very many hard cheeses. In the north of Europe there is Cheddar from Britain, for example, and in the Netherlands, Edam. Further south you can find Gruyère in Switzerland, Manchego in Spain and in Italy there is a cheese which is harder than all the others, Parmesan.

The next group is soft cheeses. The two most famous in this group are both French, Camembert and Brie.

Many countries also have another type of soft cheese, what we call a blue cheese. In Britain there is Stilton, in France Roquefort, in Italy Gorgonzola, and in Denmark Danish Blue.

Unit 12

Listening one

Wine Waiter: Would you like something to drink with your meal, sir?
Man: Yes. Now those having fish will probably prefer white wine. What about this white Lambrusco?
Wine W: That's a sparkling wine, sir.
Man: Ah, no then. What do you suggest? Something not too dry.
Wine W: I can recommend the white Bordeaux, sir. It's quite dry but very popular. Or this Rhine wine is fruity and medium dry.
Man: OK, a bottle of the Bordeaux. And now what about red? Something to please us all.
Wine W: Have you tried the house wine, sir? It's very good. Or may I suggest a Burgundy? This '83 one is excellent.
Man: Fine, we'll have the Fleurie. We can always have a carafe of the house red later.
Wine W: Thank you, sir. Will that be all?
Man: Oh, bring some mineral water, too, please.
Wine W: Certainly, sir.
Man: Well, everyone, I've chosen the wine . . .

Listening two

Man: What are the best aperitifs do you think?
Woman: It varies from country to country, but I'd say dry sparkling wine, dry white wine or Kir, and a dry or medium dry fortified wine. Oh yes, and vermouth of course.
M: With meat they say red with red and white with white. Do you think so, too?
W: Yes, a full-bodied red is best with beef and a full-bodied or light red with lamb. But I think with pork and veal a light red or a dry white is best. And rosé wine can be very good with pork.
M: I like a dry white with fish best, or perhaps a semi-dry with poached fish. You too?
W: Yes, I do.
M: And then a light red with the cheese or a full-bodied one if the cheese is strong.
W: That's right, and then a sweet white or fortified wine with the dessert or ice-cream.
M: Yes.

9 **12**

Unit 13

Listening one

Man: Waiter, could I have a knife, please?
Waiter: I'm sorry, sir. I'll get one.
Man: And we're short of a glass.
Waiter: I'll bring one, sir.

Woman: Could you bring some water, please?
Waiter: Certainly, madam.

Woman: We need another side plate, waiter.
Waiter: Yes, madam.

Woman: Can I have some French dressing?
Waitress: Yes, madam, I'll bring some.

Man: Waiter, could you bring me some cigarettes, please?
Waiter: Certainly, sir. What kind would you like?
Man: Oh, Benson and Hedges, please.

Woman: The bill, please.
Waitress: Yes, madam, I'll be right back.

Man: Waiter, have you got a light, please?
Waiter: Yes, sir. Here you are.

Woman: An ashtray, please, waiter.
Waiter: Yes, madam.

Man: Do you have any tomato sauce?
Waitress: Yes, sir. I'll get some right away.

Listening two

Head waiter: Right, Michel, well, we use the normal cover here but I want to make sure you know how to check that everything is there, and that everything's in the right place. OK?
Waiter: Yes.
Head W: The first thing to do is check that the napkin is in the plate position and correctly folded. The joint knife and fork are right and left of it.
Waiter: And the fish knife and fork outside them.
Head W: That's right, with the soup spoon to the right of the fish knife, and the dessert spoon and fork above the napkin. Then check that there is a side plate with a side knife on it to the left, and a wine glass above the soup spoon.
Waiter: And there'll be salt, pepper and an ashtray, I suppose?
Head W: That's right. They're in the middle of the table.

Unit 14

Listening one

Chef: I'm taking off the prawn cocktail from yesterday's menu and adding the smoked mackerel pâté.
Trainee: OK, that's the starters.
C: Then for fish, the new items are Sole Meunière – that's just grilled sole with melted butter – and Cod Mornay, cod steaks served with a creamy cheese sauce. For the meat, the roast of the day is pork, with all the trimmings. Steak and kidney pie is on again. Oh and Beef Stroganoff – it's a kind of stew. It's made from beef steak with mushrooms and sour cream. And the Chicken Kiev is new. It consists of chicken breasts stuffed with herbs and garlic butter, and the Tournedos are beef fillet served with sautéd bread and lemon.
T: Fine, and the vegetables?
C: Peas, French beans, spinach, carrots, and ratatouille.
T: What's in that?
C: It basically contains tomatoes, courgettes, green peppers, aubergines, and onions. Then for potatoes there's roast, French fried, new boiled, and Lyonnaise.
T: What are they?
C: Potatoes Lyonnaise? They're thin slices of potato cooked with onion in a casserole. Right, that's everything, then. Let's just run through the desserts and . . .

Listening two

OK, first you take a thin slice of veal and dip it in egg. Then you coat it in breadcrumbs and fry it. You serve it with a slice of lemon. . . . This is an unusual one because the guests do the cooking. They put cubes of good quality beef on a long fork and fry them in hot oil at the table. . . . You boil them for six or seven minutes, cut them in half, and then cover them with mayonnaise. . . . The slice of meat is grilled and served with parsley butter. . . . The fruit is first halved. The halves are poached and then covered with chocolate sauce before serving.

Unit 15

Listening one

Man: Waiter, we ordered our drinks 20 minutes ago.
Waiter: I'm terribly sorry, sir. I'll see the wine waiter for you.

Man: My steak is overdone. I asked for it rare.
Waiter: I'm sorry, sir, I'll change it for you.

Man: Waitress, this is the worst soup I've ever tasted. It's terribly salty.
Waitress: I'll take it back to the kitchen, sir. Would you like to order something else?

Woman: Waiter, you must have the slowest service in town.
Waiter: I'm sorry, madam. We're short-staffed tonight. I'll be with you in a moment.

Woman: I'm sorry, but I asked for my dessert without cream.
Waiter: So sorry, madam. One moment and I'll change it for you.

Man: I don't like to complain but this dish is completely uneatable.
Waitress: I'm sorry, sir. What exactly is wrong?
Man: The meat is completely uncooked.
Waitress: I'll speak to the chef immediately, sir. Can I bring you something else?

Man: Look at this glass, waiter. There's lipstick on it.
Waiter: My apologies, sir. I'll get you a new one.

Woman: Waiter, this is the draughtiest spot in the restaurant. Can you find us another table?
Waiter: One moment madam, I'll see what I can do.

Listening two

1
Guest: Waiter.
Waiter: Yes, sir?
Guest: This knife is dirty.
Waiter: I'm very sorry, sir. I'll get you another one.

2
Waitress: Yes, how can I help?
Guest: We've been waiting for our wine for over twenty minutes.
Waitress: I'm sorry about that sir. I'll speak to the wine waiter immediately.

3
Guest: Can we have some more butter? There's none left.
Waitress: I'll get you some, madam.

4
Waiter: Is there anything wrong, sir?
Guest: There certainly is. This fish is uneatable.
Waiter: What's the problem, sir?
Guest: Well, to start with it's undercooked, and then it's cold, too.
Waiter: I'm sorry about that. I'll have it replaced.

Unit 16

Listening one

All the food for the restaurant is prepared and cooked in this kitchen. Fresh bread, rolls and croissants are baked daily on the premises. The pastry cook also prepares all the hot desserts and a variety of Danish pastries and petits fours . . .

All the ovens and hobs are here behind the preparation areas. The assistant chef works here on the line. He's responsible for all the side orders, hot soups, and hot starters. He's got his own commis to help him . . .

This is your station here with me on all the meat, fish and pasta items. We do roasts, grills, stews, poached fish, and sauces for the pasta. You'll also help the other commis with the salads and cold first courses . . .

These are the refrigerators here and this is the walk-in cold store. This is the dish table. You slide the dish racks along and into the dishwasher. Those are the heat lamps over there where the food is checked and kept hot before the waiters take it into the dining-room.

We supply all the knives. You'll need to sharpen them daily. Sieves, colanders, ladles, and wooden spoons are kept here at the line chef's station. The mincers, blenders, whisks, and other utensils are there at the end . . .

If you are on the early shift, you start at seven and finish at three with a one-hour break . . .

Listening two

Visitor: We use pans like these in France, too, but I don't know what they're called.
Chef: Well, I'll tell you the English names, if you like.
V: Fine.
C: The most normal type of pan is the saucepan. We use them for many things – not just sauces.
V: That big one there with the two small handles. Is that a saucepan too?
C: No, we call that a stockpot. We use it for boiling meat bones and vegetables to make stock.
V: I see. The low one with a handle is a frying-pan, isn't it?
C: That's right, and that's a baking-tin next to it, the one with no handles. That just leaves two more – the soufflé dish, with high sides, and the flan or tart dish with the low sides. We use a lot of French in kitchen English, as you can hear.
V: Good, that'll be a help.

Unit 17

Listening one

Commis: So where do you want me to start?
Chef: First we have to organize the roasts. Light the ovens and get them to the right temperature. There's pork and lamb today so get the baking tins and fat ready. I'll get the meat.
Commis: What's this for?
Chef: That's the list of vegetables for the day. Can you go to the cold store and get them, and I'll see to the meat. Then I'll explain what to do . . .

Commis: OK, I think that's the lot.
Chef: Right, first peel the potatoes and carrots. Then julienne the carrots and celery and prepare the broccoli, sprouts, and French beans. We blanch all the vegetables now and then sauté them to order in clarified butter.
Commis: What's that?
Chef: Melted butter with all the water removed. I'll see to that today. You start on the vegetables. Then there's apple sauce for the pork. Peel and chop those apples and when you've cooked them put them through the sieve to make a purée. The lamb is with garlic and rosemary. I'll do that.
Commis: Is that it?
Chef: No, there's a veal ragout, and roast and duchesse potatoes to do, and the fish to be poached. Can you chop the veal and then go on to the Chef's salad?
Commis: What's in that?
Chef: Use the crisp lettuce, watercress, radishes, and fennel. Oh, and you'll have to whisk up some fresh mayonnaise. Mix in a little lemon juice with the olive oil and egg yolks. You mustn't do it too quickly or it curdles.

Listening two

OK, let's get moving. Mary, you can stop kneading that dough. Leave it on the side for a minute. I need you to peel and julienne these carrots first. Martin, chop those onions and then fry them, will you? Then you can mix them with that steak that you minced a few minutes ago. Toby, those boiled potatoes must be ready by now. You can strain them and leave then to keep warm in the bain-marie. When you've done that you can grill the chops. Look out for that sauce – it's starting to curdle – give it a good whisk. OK so far, now let's . . .

Unit 18

Listening one

Reception: Reception.
Guest: Can I have room service, please?
Recep: One moment, madam, and I'll put you through.
Room Service: Room Service, can I help you?
Guest: Hello, am I too late to order from the breakfast menu?
Room S: No, madam, the room service menu is on twenty-four hours a day.
Guest: Good, then can I have one English breakfast?
Room S: Cereal or fruit juice, madam?
Guest: Fruit juice, please.
Room S: And either tea or coffee?
Guest: Tea. Also, a beefburger with French fries, no onions; a ham sandwich, and two tuna and salad sandwiches.
Room S: One burger and fries, one ham and two tuna sandwiches. Anything else, madam?
Guest: Some drinks, please. Two strawberry milk shakes, and a hot chocolate.
Room S: Two strawberry shakes and one hot chocolate. Right. What room number, please?
Guest: Room 328.
Room S: 328. Thank you, madam.

Listening two

1
Caller: Hallo, can I speak to Mr Lubitch?
Reception: That's room 612. I'll call for you. . . . There's no answer. Can I give him a message?
Caller: Yes, this is René Leblanc. Can you tell him I'll be one hour late for our meeting tonight?
Recep: Yes, of course.

2
Caller: Mary Anderson, please.
Reception: I'm afraid she's gone out. Can I help you?
Caller: Yes, tell her I'll call her before 9 tomorrow morning.
Recep: Certainly. What name shall I give?
Caller: Oh yes, Miss Burton, Christine Burton.

3
Caller: Can you put me through to Peter Schmidt?
Reception: He went out about an hour ago. Can I take a message?
Caller: Yes, this is the Globe Travel Agency. Could you tell him his ticket's ready?

Unit 19

Listening one

Reservations: Good morning, Park Hotel. Can I help you? (*zzzzzzzz crackle zzzzzzzz*) Hallo, we seem to have a very bad line. Can you speak up a little?
Caller: My name is Dreyton. I'd like to . . .
Res: That's better. Could you spell your name, please?
Caller: D-R-E-Y-T-O-*
Res: I'm sorry, I didn't catch the last letter.
Caller: N.
Res: Did you say 'N' for Norway?
Caller: That's right. I'd like to make a reservation.
Res: Yes, Mr Dreyton. When for?
Caller: For * nights from July *
Res: I'm sorry, could you repeat that?
Caller: For three nights from July *
Res: July the?
Caller: Tenth.
Res: From July 10th. Is it just for yourself?
Caller: No for me and my *. We'd like two double rooms.
Res: Excuse me, I didn't catch that. This line's really bad.
Caller: There are four of us. We'd like two double rooms.
Res: Two double rooms for three nights from July 10th. Is that right?
Caller: Yes. what's the address of the hotel?.
Res: It's 30 Bewlay Place. I'll spell that. B-E-W-L-A-Y. London W.1. Can I have your telephone number?
Caller: I'm calling from Bologna in Italy. The area code is 51 and then 29 31 05.
Res: 09?
Caller: No, 05.
Res: 51 29 31 05. Thank you, Mr Dreyton. We'll hold the rooms until 6 pm . . .

Listening two

G-O-N-Z-A-L-E-Z
J-O-H-N-S-O-N
P-A-T-R-E-L-L-I
T-H-E-O-D-O-R-A-K-I-S
D-U-V-A-L
E-R-I-K-S-S-O-N
T-E-L-L
L-A-U-D-R-U-P
V-A-N D-E V-E-E-N
J-A-N-S-S-E-N
G-I-L-B-A-O
S-C H-M-I-D-T

Unit 20

Listening one

1

Guest: My dinner-jacket needs cleaning and pressing, and I need to wear it this evening.

Reception: That's OK sir. Somebody'll pick up the jacket from your room and we'll have it ready for you by 5. Which room are you in?

2

Guest: Hallo, does the hotel have a clothes repair service?

Reception: One moment, madam, I'll put you through to the Housekeeper.

Housekeeper: Housekeeping.

Guest: Hallo, I need a couple of buttons sewn on a blouse. Can you do it for me today?

Hskpr: We can do it by tomorrow morning, madam. Will that be all right?

Guest: Fine, I don't need it till mid-morning. Shall I leave it with the hall porter?

Hskpr: You needn't, madam. I'll send someone up for it straight away. What room number is it?

3

Reception: Reception.

Guest: Hallo. My wife has some jewellery that we're afraid to leave in our room. Is there somewhere you could keep it for us?

Recep: Certainly, sir. Bring the valuables down to me. I'll write you a receipt for them, and we'll put them in the safe in the manager's office.

Listening two

Guest: What about a haircut? Do you have someplace I can get one?

Reception: Yes, sir, we certainly do. The hairdressing salon is on the other side of the foyer and it's open from 9 am to 5 pm every day of the week.

Guest: Good, . . . oh and I need to change my airline reservation.

Recep: There's a travel agency next to the hotel, open from 9 to 5.

Guest: Fine, and dollars, I need to change a few dollars.

Recep: No problem, sir, there's an exchange bureau next to the hairdressing salon.

Guest: Does it happen to be open now?

Recep: Yes, indeed. It's open from 8 am to midnight daily, sir. So you have plenty of time.

Guest: And a coffee shop?

Recep: There is one, yes, open 24 hours a day. Can you see the lifts? It's over there behind them.

Guest: You mean the elevators?

Recep: Yes, that's right. Behind them.

Unit 21

Listening one

1

Visitor: Which room is Mr Moreau in?

Hall Porter: He's in room 208.

Visitor: How do I find 208?

Hall Porter: Take the lift to the second floor. Turn right when you come out of the lift, walk along the corridor and you'll see it on the right.

2

Guest: Excuse me, where's the coffee shop?.

Hall Porter: It's on this floor. Just go across the lobby, through that doorway and then down the corridor. You'll see it at the end of the corridor, facing you.

3

Guest: Can I buy stamps in the hotel?

Chambermaid: Yes, madam, at the gift shop on the ground floor. It's at the bottom of the main staircase opposite the reception desk.

4

Guest: I'm looking for conference room B.

Chambermaid: Yes, sir. It's on the top floor. When you come out of the lift, turn right. Go past the stairs to the roof garden, turn left, and the conference suite is immediately on your right.

5

Guest: Where's the hairdressing salon, please?

Hall Porter: It's in the basement, madam. Go through that door on the other side of the foyer and then down the stairs. Turn right along the corridor and you'll see the salon in front of you.

Listening two

Housekeeper: OK, when you check the room, make sure that there are enough hangers in the wardrobe. Some guests take them, you know. Oh and check the mini-bar is full – you have the list of what it's supposed to contain, don't you? – and that the air-conditioning is set correctly.

New Maid: Right, I'll do that. Do all rooms have the same equipment?

Hskpr: Yes, there are always one or two beds, which means one or two bedside tables and armchairs as well. Then there's a dressing-table, a chest of drawers, and a TV. Oh, and a stool for the dressing-table, too. I think that's about all.

New M: And they all have both curtains and a blind?

Hskpr: Yes. Make sure the curtains are open and the blind up before the guests come in. And one other thing, if you find . . .

Unit 22

Listening one

1

Guest: Have you got a map of the city centre?

Hall Porter: Yes, madam. Here you are.

Guest: We'd like to go to the art gallery this morning. Is it far from here?

Hall P: About ten minutes' walk.

Guest: Can you direct us there?

Hall P: Certainly, madam. Open up your map a moment and I'll show you where it is. Turn left outside the hotel, go down to the traffic lights, and turn right. Carry on down Union Street past the railway station until you can't go any further – it's this T junction here. Then turn left and you'll see the art gallery about 100 metres along on your right. Just here.

Guest: That's kind of you. Thank you.

2

Guest: What's the quickest way to the zoo from here?

Doorman: Get the number 19 bus from the bus station, sir. You can get off right outside the zoo.

Guest: And where's the bus station?

Doorman: Not far. Just cross this street and go down to the roundabout. Use the subway and take the Bridge Street exit. Then go down Bridge Street and over the bridge and you'll see the bus station straight ahead of you.

3

Guest: Excuse me, is there a post office near here?

Hall Porter: About five minutes on foot, madam. Turn right outside the hotel. Go straight over at the traffic lights. Then take the second left, and the first right, and you're there. It's in Middle Street.

Listening two

1

German: Excuse me, can you tell me how to get from Euston to Harrods, please?

Londoner: Yes, of course. Er, you'll want the Victoria line first. That'll take you to Green Park. Change onto the Piccadilly line there and it's only two stations to Knightsbridge which is where you get off for Harrods.

German: Fine, thank you very much.

2

American: I need to get from here to Victoria by subway. Can you tell me how I do that?

Londoner: Certainly. Take the Central line as far as Oxford Circus and change onto the Victoria line there. After that it's only two stops and you're at Victoria station.

American: Great, that sounds real easy.

3

Italian: Excuse me, can you tell me the way to the National Gallery?

Londoner: Well, it's too far to walk. You'll need to take the underground.

Italian: Yes, fine. Which way do I go?

Londoner: There are two ways. You can take the Central line to Tottenham Court Road, and then the Northern line to Charing Cross. Then you have to walk across Trafalgar Square to the gallery. Or you could take the Circle line to the Embankment, and walk from there. You don't have to change but the walk's a bit longer.

Italian: OK, thanks.

Unit 23

Listening one

Guest 1: Yes, we really are enjoying our stay. It's a lovely city.

Hall Porter: Good, it's the best time of year here. What have you planned for today, Mrs Johnson?

Guest 1: We thought we'd visit the modern art exhibition at the art gallery. Have you heard anything about it?

Hall P: I believe it's very good. They have exhibits there from all over the world. You ought to visit the permanent exhibition, too. They have some wonderful old masters there.

Guest 2: Excuse me, can you help? My husband has just fallen on the steps outside the hotel. I think he may have broken something.

Hall P: Oh dear. I'll send a porter out right away and we'll bring him in here.

Porter: We'll have you comfortable in just a moment, Mr Lascelles. There we are.

Guest 2: Will you call a doctor for us?

Hall P: Yes, madam. But I think you should have an ambulance to take him into casualty. The doctor will certainly need an X-ray and that wound may need dressing.

Guest 2: Yes, I suppose so.

Hall P: I'll phone right away, Mrs Lascelles. Oh Jim, have you finished that job in 126?

Porter: Yes, Mr Maunders.

Hall P: Then go to the chemists with this prescription for 188, will you?

Porter: OK, Mr Maunders.

Listening two

1

Man: Waiter, I'm not feeling at all well. I'm very dizzy.

Waiter: Why don't you come out to the back and lie down. I'll call a doctor.

Man: Yes, if you can just help me . . .

2

Woman: I'm sorry to trouble you, but I've got a problem. My handbag is broken. You see, here, the strap has broken.

Reception: Ah yes, I see. Why don't you take it to the shoemaker's across the road? I'm sure he'll fix it for you in no time.

Woman: Oh, good, yes. Thanks for your help.

3

Reception: Can I help you? Is something wrong?

Woman: Yes, I've got a terrible toothache.

Recep: I'm sorry to hear that. Have you taken a painkiller at all?

Woman: No, I haven't got any.

Recep: Well, I'll give you a couple of aspirin and then I'll call the emergency dentist for you.

Woman: Yes, will you do that? Thanks.

Unit 24

Listening one

1

Reception: Reception.

Guest: This is Mr Graham in 324. I've just checked in.

Recep: Ah, yes, Mr Graham. What can I do for you?

Guest: Well, my room obviously hasn't been cleaned since the last guest. The carpet's dirty, the bed's unmade, and the bathroom hasn't been touched.

Recep: I'm terribly sorry, sir. Housekeeping should've seen to everything this morning. I'll contact them straight away and I'll send someone up to see you . . .

2

Reception: Reception.

Guest: This is room 632. Our room isn't ready for us. There are no towels, soap or toilet paper in the bathroom.

Recep: I'm so sorry, madam. These things should've been ready for you. I'll contact housekeeping straight away. . .

3

Reception: Reception.

Guest: Can you do something about the shower in my room? It's only running cold water.

Recep: I'm sorry, sir. I'll send someone up to look at it. What's your room number?

Guest: 417. And the light bulb in my bedside lamp doesn't work.

Recep: Right, sir. I'll send up a new bulb, too.

4

Reception: Reception.

Guest: This is room 301. The noise in 302 next door to me is awful. I can't sleep. Can you do something about it?

Recep: Of course, sir. I'll speak to the people there straight away.

Listening two

Seventy years ago, the Carlton Hotel in London had the most famous restaurant in the world under a chef called Georges Auguste Escoffier. Many young chefs trained there and carried the excellence of French cuisine to countries all over the world. Escoffier started cooking at his uncle's restaurant in Nice in 1859, when he was thirteen. At nineteen he moved to Paris to the famous Petit Moulin Rouge. He stayed there for many years, married, and had two sons and a daughter. In 1884 he moved to Monte Carlo as Directeur de Cuisine at the Grand Hotel and in the summer he worked in the Hotel National in Lucerne, Switzerland. Here he met César Ritz and in 1890 they both went to London to manage the Savoy Hotel there. Later they opened the Ritz in Paris and the Carlton in London.

When he was seventy-three years old, Escoffier returned to Monte Carlo but still worked for another fifteen years. Towards the end of his life he was especially famous in Copenhagen, Stockholm, Frankfurt, Zurich, Prague and New York. His book 'Le Guide Culinaire' still contains all that is best in Classical French and International cookery.

Unit 25

Listening one

1
Guest: I'll be checking out this morning. Can you prepare my bill, please?
Reception: It's all ready for you, madam.
Guest: Oh good, then I'll settle it now.
Recep: How are you paying, madam?
Guest: I'd like to pay by credit card. Is that OK?
Recep: Certainly, madam. Here you are.
Guest: This all looks OK. Is service included?
Recep: Yes, service and Value Added Tax are included in the total. Would you just sign here, please?
Guest: Fine, here's my card.
Recep: And now your signature again here. Thank you. Here's your receipt.

2
Guest: Could I have the bill, please?
Waiter: Yes, sir, I'll be right with you . . . Here we are, sir, your bill.
Guest: Thank you, I'd like to pay by cheque.

Waiter: Do you have a banker's card?
Guest: Yes.
Waiter: That's fine then, sir.
Guest: Have you included the drinks from the bar?
Waiter: Yes, they're at the top – there.
Guest: Ah yes. Who shall I make the cheque out to?
Waiter: Don't worry, sir. I'll stamp it for you.
Guest: Is service included?
Waiter: No, sir.
Guest: Then I'll make the cheque out for £3 more.
Waiter: Thank you very much, sir.
Guest: Could you give me a receipt?

Listening two

1
Guest: Good morning, my name's Johnson, room 207. I'd like to pay, please. You do take Mastercard, don't you?
Cashier: Yes, we do. If you'd like to . . .

2
Cashier: What room number, sir?
Guest: 317.
Cashier: Ah yes, Mr Watanabe. How are you paying?
Guest: With dollar traveller's cheques, if that's OK.
Cashier: Fine, sir, that'll be . . .

3
Cashier: That's the total payable at the bottom, Mrs Schneider.
Guest: Fine. I'd like to pay by Eurocheque, please.
Cashier: Yes, of course, madam. Will you just . . .

4
Guest: . . . and I'd like to pay in cash, Swiss francs.
Cashier: Certainly, Mr Williams. The amount in Swiss francs is . . .

Unit 26

Listening one

1

Guest: I'd like to settle my bill now please.
Reception: Here you are, madam.
Guest: What's this item please?
Recep: That's for the telephone calls.
Guest: It can't be right. I didn't make many calls. It seems far too much money.
Recep: Just a moment madam. I'll check it for you. 630 units at 10 cents a unit is 63 dollars. I'm afraid there's no mistake.
Guest: What about this? You've got me down for dinner on four nights. I wasn't here the night of the 6th.
Recep: I beg your pardon, that's a mistake. I'll just put it through the computer again . . .

2

Waitress: Your bill, sir.
Guest: Thank you. Can I pay in Deutschmarks?
Waitress: Yes, sir. That'll be OK. We accept Deutschmarks, dollars, pounds sterling or French francs.
Guest: I think there's a mistake. We didn't have smoked salmon or so much wine.
Waitress: One moment sir. I'm sorry this isn't your bill. The cashier has confused you with another table. I'll get you the right bill. I'm sorry about that.

Guest: This looks about right . . .

Listening two

OK, on this bill the guest's name is Jarman, Mrs Jarman. You can see that in the top left-hand corner. Below the name is the deposit paid, in this case nothing. The room number, as you can see, is 318 and the rate £60. Then, moving to the right, you've got the other important details: number of guests, in this case two, and so on. For each day the guest stays, the computer will give the date, the word 'apartments' and the room rate amount under 'charges'. In this case the guests were on a package tour and the tour company, Sunshine Holidays, paid £120 to us. This goes under 'credits'. The computer then calculates the balance, which in this case is zero, of course.

Unit 27

Listening one

1

Reception: Here's your receipt sir. I hope you enjoyed your stay.
Guest: We did very much thank you. We're ready now for the next stage of our trip. We're flying to Florida tonight. We're going to see our daughter there.
Recep: Shall I get a porter to help you with your luggage?
Guest: No, thank you. I think we can manage.
Recep: Ah, this looks like your taxi now.
Guest: If we're in Lyon again we'll certainly stay here.
Recep: Have a pleasant trip and safe journey.
Guest: Goodbye.

2

Man: I think that's right, waiter, and this is for you.
Waiter: Thank you very much, sir. I'll get your coats for you. Is this one yours, madam?
Woman: Yes.
Waiter: And yours, sir.
Man: Thank you. Goodbye.

Man: Ah waiter, I've forgotten my briefcase. I think I left it down by my chair. The table by the window.
Waiter: I'll get it for you, sir.
Man: Oh good. Our plane leaves at midnight. I'd be lost without it. Thanks. Goodbye again.
Waiter: Goodbye.

Listening two

1

Guest: Well, we'll certainly stay here next time we're passing through.
Reception: Good, do let us know in advance, and we'll try to get you the same room.
Guest: That would be lovely. It may be quite soon, in fact.
Recep: Oh, how's that?
Guest: Well, we're driving to the south of Spain in the next couple of days, and we may come back this way.
Recep: Do give us a ring if you decide to. I hope you have a pleasant trip.

2

Maître d'hôtel: Your taxi's here, sir.

Guest: Oh, fine. We're a bit late for the theatre. Too much of your excellent food again, Gaston.

M. d': I'm glad you enjoyed it, sir. I hope we'll see you again soon.

Guest: I'm sure you will.

3

Guest: How long does it take to get to the airport?

Reception: About an hour on the underground.

Guest: Oh, that'll do us fine. No point in wasting money on a taxi. How early is the check-in time for British Airways?

Recep: Well, it depends. Where are you going?

Guest: Helsinki.

Recep: In that case, it's only 30 minutes before the departure time.

Guest: Well, we'd better be going anyway.

Unit 28

Listening one

Interviewer: Good morning. Please come in and sit down.

Martine: Thank you.

I: I'd like to take down a few personal details first. What's your name?

M: Miss Nouveau. Martine Nouveau.

I: And your address?

M: 51 rue du Faubourg St. Antoine, 75011 Paris.

I: Are you on the telephone?

M: Yes. My home number is 48-37-25-06.

I: Your date of birth, please.

M: August 22nd 1967.

I: And you're not married, are you?

M: That's right.

I: Now, you're applying for the job of receptionist at one of our hotels in the city centre.

M: Yes.

I: What qualifications do you have?

M: I've done the BEP course and I did one year of BTS.

I: Do you speak any foreign languages?

M: Some English. I've studied for four years. And a little German.

I: I see. What experience do you have in hotel work?

M: As a student I worked for two summers in the kitchens of the Constantin, and since I left college 18 months ago, I've been in a small hotel in the 16th – the Roi du Soleil – mainly in reception and also helping in the dining-room.

I: Have you had any other jobs?

M: Just some part-time shop work.

I: And when are you available from?

M: I have to give one week's notice.

I: Well, Miss Nouveau, thank you for coming along. I'll let you know as soon as possible if we can offer you a job. We finish interviewing in a few days, so . . .

Listening two

My name is Jean Laval and I was born 20 years ago in Geneva, where I still live, at 16 rue Rousseau. When I finished school I went to the Hotel and Restaurant College and studied there for three years before I got my chef's certificate. Then I started work in a restaurant here in Geneva, Chez Nico. I have worked here as a commis for about a year. I have enjoyed it but the restaurant is a small one with a small menu and I think I have got all the experience I can here. So now I want to move on. It may be necessary to travel away from Geneva or even outside Switzerland, but that's OK. The best place for me would be a big, high-class restaurant in a big city or maybe in a five star hotel. It has to be a big place so that I'll get lots of new experience . . .

26 28

ENGLISH AND AMERICAN ENGLISH	FRENCH	ITALIAN	SPANISH
above 13	au-dessus de	sopra	encima de
accept 26	accepter	accettare	aceptar
add 7	ajouter	aggiungere	añadir
address 19 (*noun*)	adresse	indirizzo	dirección
advertise 28 (*verb*)	mettre une annonce dans la presse	mettere un'inserzione sul giornale	anunciar
advertisement 28	annonce	inserzione	anuncio
air-conditioning 21	climatisation	aria condizionata	aire acondicionado
à la carte 2	à la carte	à la carte	a la carta
all right 7	d'accord	va bene	está bien
alphabet 19	alphabet	alfabeto	alfabeto
always 7	toujours	sempre	siempre
a.m. 3	du matin	di mattina	por la mañana
ambulance 23	ambulance	ambulanza	ambulancia
amount 25 (*noun*)	montant	importo	importe
another 13	un autre	un altro	otro
answer 4 (*verb*)	répondre	risposta	contestar
applicant 28	candidat	candidato	candidato
application form 28	formulaire	modulo di domanda	hoja de solicitud
apology 15	excuses	scuse	disculpas
area 10	région	zona	región
area code 19	indicatif	prefisso (in teleselezione)	indicativo/prefijo
armchair 21	fauteuil	poltrona	butaca
art gallery 22	galerie d'art	galleria d'arte	galeria de arte
ashtray 13	cendrier	portacenere	cenicero
assistant 16	aide-	aiutante	asistente
assorted 18	assorti	assortito	variado
aubergine 9 (**US**: eggplant)	aubergine	melanzana	berenjena
available 20	disponible	disponibile	disponible
avocado pear 8	avocat (fruit)	avocado	aguacate
awful 24	affreux	terribile	horrible

bacon 18	lard	pancetta (affumicata)	tocino
bain-marie 17 (**US**: double boiler)	bain-marie	bagnomaria	al baño-maría
baking-tin 16 (**US**: baking pan)	plat à four	vassoio da forno	bandeja
balance 26 (*noun*)	solde	saldo	saldo
banker's card 25 (**US**: bank card)	carte bancaire	carta bancaria	tarjeta del banco
bar 2	bar	bar	bar
bar steward 7 (**US**: bartender)	barman	barman	camarero
basement 21	sous-sol	seminterrato	sótano
basket 11	panier	cestino	cesta
bath 21	bain	bagno	baño
batter 14	pâte à frire	pastella	batido (para rebozar)
beauty salon 21	institut de beauté	istituto di bellezza	salón de belleza
bedside table 21 (**US**: night stand)	table de nuit	comodino	mesita de noche
beefburger 18 (**US**: hamburger)	hamburger	hamburger	hamburguesa
believe 23	croire	credere	creer
below 7	au-dessous de	sotto	debajo/abajo
bill 13 (*noun*)	addition	conto	cuenta
biscuit 11 (**US**: cookie)	biscuit	biscotto	galleta
bitter 6 (**US**: beer)	brune (bière)	birra scura	amargo
blanch 17	blanchir	scottare	bañar con agua hirviendo
blender 16	mixer	mescolatore	batidora
blind 21 (*noun*)	store	veneziana	persiana
blouse 20	chemisier	camicetta	blusa

Word List

ENGLISH AND AMERICAN ENGLISH	GERMAN	GREEK
above 13	oberhalb	από πάνω/πάνω από
accept 26	akzeptieren	δέχομαι
add 7	hinzufügen	προσθέτω
address 19 (noun)	Addresse	διεύθυνση
advertise 28 (verb)	ausschreiben	διαφημίζω
advertisement 28	Anzeige	διαφήμηση,αγγελία
air-conditioning 21	Klimaanlage	κλιματισμός
à la carte 2	à la carte	αλα κάρτ
all right 7	okay	εντάξει
alphabet 19	Alphabet	αλφάβητο
always 7	immer	πάντοτε
a.m. 3	morgens	π.μ. (προ μεσημβρίας)
ambulance 23	Krankenwagen	ασθενφόρο
amount 25 (noun)	Betrag	ποσό
another 13	noch ein; ein(e) andere (r, s)	άλλο ένα/ακόμη ένα
answer 4 (verb)	antworten	απαντώ
applicant 28	Bewerber(in)	αιτών
application form 28	Bewerbungsformular	έντυπη αίτηση
apology 15	Entschuldigung	(αίτηση για) συγγνώμη
area 10	Gebiet	περιοχή
area code 19	Vorwahl	ταχυδρομικός τομέας
armchair 21	Sessel	πολυθρόνα
art gallery 22	Kunstgalerie	γκαλλερί τέχνης
ashtray 13	Aschenbecher	τασάκι
assistant 16	Assistenz-	βοηθός
assorted 18	gemischt	διάφορα/ποικιλία από (π.χ.τυριά)
aubergine 9 (US: eggplant)	Aubergine	μελιτζάνα
available 20	erhältlich	διαθέσιμος
avocado pear 8	Avocado	αβοκάντο
awful 24	schrecklich	φρικτός
bacon 18	Speck	μπέηκον
bain-marie 17 (US: double boiler)	Wasserbad	μπαίν μαρί
baking-tin 16 (US: baking pan)	Backform	ταψί/λαμαρίνα φούρνου
balance 26 (noun)	Saldo	υπόλοιπο
banker's card 25 (US: bank card)	Scheckkarte	τραπεζική κάρτα
bar 2	Bar	μπάρ
bar steward 7 (US: bartender)	Barkeeper	μπάρμαν
basement 21	Untergeschoß	υπόγειο
basket 11	Korb	καλάθι
bath 21	Badewanne	μπάνιο
batter 14	Teig	κουρκούτι
beauty salon 21	Kosmetiksalon	ινστιτούτο αισθητικής
bedside table 21 (US: night stand)	Nachttisch	κομοδίνο
beefburger 18 (US: hamburger)	Hamburger	μπιφτέκι
believe 23	glauben	πιστεύω
below 7	unterhalb	παρακάτω
bill 13 (noun)	Rechnung	λογαριασμός
biscuit 11 (US: cookie)	Keks	μπισκότο
bitter 6 (US: beer)	Bitter (Bier)	πικρή (μπύρα)
blanch 17	blanchieren	ζεματίζω
blender 16	Mixgerät	ηλεκτρικός αναμίκτης/μπλέντερ
blind 21 (noun)	Jalousie	στόρι (παραθύρου)
blouse 20	Bluse	μπλούζα (γυναικεία)

ENGLISH AND AMERICAN ENGLISH	FRENCH	ITALIAN	SPANISH
boil 14	faire bouillir	bollire	hervir
bones 16	os	ossa	huesos
book 1 (*verb*)	réserver	prenotare	reservar
bottle 8	bouteille	bottiglia	botella
bottled 6	mis en bouteille	imbottigliato	embotellar
bottom 21	fond	fondo	parte inferior
bowl 24 (*for sugar*)	sucrier	zuccheriera	cuenco
brandy 6	eau de vie	cognac	coñac
bread 8	pain	pane	pan
breadcrumbs 14	chapelure	pangrattato	pan rallado
break 23 (*verb*)	casser	rompere	romper
breast 14 (*chicken*)	blanc (de poulet)	petto (di pollo)	pechuga
bridge 22	pont	ponte	puente
briefcase 27	serviette	cartella	cartera
bring 13	apporter	portare	traer
broken 7	cassé	rotto	roto
bucket 11 (*for wine*)	seau à glace	secchio	balde/cubo
bulb 24	ampoule (électrique)	lampadina	bombilla
bureau 20	agence	ufficio	agencia
Burgundy 10	Bourgogne	vino di Borgogna	Borgoña
bus 22	autobus	autobus	autobús
busy 4	occupé	pieno di lavoro	ocupado
butter 9	beurre	burro	mantequilla
button 20	bouton	bottone	botón
calculate 18	calculer	calcolare	calcular
car 5	voiture/auto	automobile	coche
car park 2 (**US:** parking lot)	parking	parcheggio	aparcamiento
carafe 12	carafe	caraffa	garrafa
carpet 24	moquette	tappeto	alfombra
cash 20 (*verb*)	encaisser (chèque)	cambiare	en efectivo
cashier 26	caissier	cassiere	cajero
castle 22	château fort	castello	castillo
Casualty 23	Urgences	Pronto Soccorso	Servicio de Urgencia
catch 19 (*verb i.e. to hear*)	bien entendre/comprendre	afferrare	captar
cathedral 22	cathédrale	duomo	catedral
centre 2 (**US:** center)	centre	centro	centro
cereal 18	céréales	cereali	cereales
change 15 (*verb*)	changer	cambiare	cambiar
charge 6 (*verb*)	mettre sur (mon) compte	addebitare	cobrar
Charlotte Russe 11	Charlotte Russe	charlotte	carlota rusa
cheap 10	bon marché	economico	barato
check 13	vérifier	controllare	comprobar
check in 24 (*verb*)	remplir une fiche (d'hôtel)	registrare all'albergo	registrarse
check out 25 (*verb*)	régler sa note et partir	saldare il conto e partire	pagar la factura y marcharse
cheese 9	fromage	formaggio	queso
cheese board 11	plateau de fromage	selezione di formaggi	bandeja de quesos
cheese-cake 11	flan au fromage blanc	torta di ricotta	pastel de queso
chemist's 23 (**US:** pharmacist's)	pharmacie	farmacia	farmacia
cheque 25 (**US:** check)	chèque	assegno	cheque
chest of drawers 21 (**US:** dresser)	commode	cassettone	comoda
chill 7 (*verb*)	refroidir	raffreddare	enfriar
chocolate gateau 11	gâteau au chocolat	torta di cioccolato	torta de chocolate
chop 17 (*verb*)	hacher	tagliare a pezzetti	cortar/picar
cider 6	cidre	sidro	sidra
cinema 22 (**US:** movie theatre)	cinéma	cinema	cine
city 2	(grande) ville	città	ciudad

WORD LIST

ENGLISH AND AMERICAN ENGLISH	GERMAN	GREEK
boil 14	kochen	βράζω
bones 16	Knochen	κόκκαλα
book 1 (*verb*)	reservieren	κάνω κράτηση/κλείνω
bottle 8	Flasche	μποτίλια
bottled 6	in Flaschen	εμφιαλωμένο
bottom 21	Ende	στο κάτω μέρος
bowl 24 (*for sugar*)	Schale	μπώλ
brandy 6	Weinbrand	κονιάκ/μπράντυ
bread 8	Brot	ψωμί
breadcrumbs 14	Paniermehl	ψίχουλα
break 23 (*verb*)	brechen	σπάζω
breast 14 (*chicken*)	Brüstchen	στήθος (κοτόπουλο)
bridge 22	Brücke	γέφυρα
briefcase 27	Aktentasche	χαρτοφύλακας
bring 13	bringen	φέρνω
broken 7	zerstoßen	σπασμένος
bucket 11 (*for wine*)	Kübel	σαμπανιέρα
bulb 24	Glühbirne	λαμπτήρας
bureau 20	Büro	γραφείο
Burgundy 10	Burgunder	Βουργουνδία
bus 22	Bus	λεωφορείο
busy 4	geschäftig/lebhaft	φορτωμένος/ πολυάσχολος
butter 9	Butter	βούτυρο
button 20	Knopf	κουμπί

calculate 18	errechnen	υπολογίζω
car 5	Auto	αυτοκίνητο
car park 2 (**US**: parking lot)	Parkplatz	πάρκνγκ
carafe 12	Karaffe	καράφα
carpet 24	Teppich	χαλί
cash 20 (*verb*)	einlösen	εξαργυρώνω
cashier 26	Kassierer(in)	ταμίας
castle 22	Schloß	κάστρο
Casualty 23	Unfallstation	Πρώτες Βοήθειες
catch 19 (*verb i.e. to hear*)	mitbekommen	'το πιάνω' =ακούω
cathedral 22	Kathedrale	μητρόπολη/καθεδρικός ναός
centre 2 (**US**: center)	Zentrum	κέντρο
cereal 18	Cerealien	δημητριακά
change 15 (*verb*)	austauschen	αλλάζω
charge 6 (*verb*)	auf die Rechnung setzen	χρεώνω
Charlotte Russe 11	Charlotte russe	Σαρλότ Ρους
cheap 10	billig	φτηνός
check 13	überprüfen	ελέγχω
check in 24 (*verb*)	sich anmelden	υπογράφω κατά την άφιξη
check out 25 (*verb*)	abreisen	υπογράφω κατά την αναχώρηση
cheese 9	Käse	τυρί
cheese board 11	Käseplatte	δίσκος με τυριά
cheese-cake 11	Käsekuchen	τσήζκεϊκ (γλυκό με τυρί)
chemist's 23 (**US**: pharmacist's)	Apotheke	φαρμακείο
cheque 25 (**US**: check)	Scheck	επιταγή
chest of drawers 21 (**US**: dresser)	Kommode	κομμό
chill 7 (*verb*)	kühlen	παγώνω
chocolate gateau 11	Schokoladentorte	τούρτα σοκολάτα
chop 17 (*verb*)	kleinschneiden	ψιλοκόβω
cider 6	Cidre	μηλίτης (κρασί)
cinema 22 (**US**: movie theatre)	Kino	κινηματογράφος
city 2	City	πόλη/μεγαλούπολη

WORD LIST

ENGLISH AND AMERICAN ENGLISH	FRENCH	ITALIAN	SPANISH
claret 10	vin de Bordeaux	vino di Bordeaux	vino de Bordeos
clarified butter 17	beurre clarifié	burro raffinato	mantequilla fundida
clean 20 (*verb*)	nettoyer	pulire	limpiar
close 3 (*verb*)	fermer	chiudere	cerrar
clothes 20	vêtements	abiti	ropa
coat 5	manteau	soprabito	abrigo
cocktail 7	cocktail	cocktail	cóctel
cocktail shaker 7	shaker	shaker	coctelera
cod 9	cabillaud	merluzzo	bacalao
coffee shop 2	café/cafétéria	cafe	cafetería
colander 16	passoire	colino	colador
cold store 16	chambre froide	cella frigorifera	cámara frigorífica
college 27	établissement d'enseignement sup.	collegio	colegio
comfortable 23	confortable	comodo	cómodo
commis 16 (**US**: junior)	commis	addetto ai servizi di cucina	funcionario
company 26	société	compagnia	sociedad
complain 15	se plaindre	lamentarsi	quejarse
computer 18	ordinateur	computer	computadora/ordenador
conference 21	conférence	conferenza	conferencia/congreso
confused 26	confus	confuso	confuso
cooked 9	cuit	cotto	cocido
copy 28 (*noun*)	copie	copia	copia
corkscrew 11	tire-bouchon	cavatappi	sacacorchos
corner 26 (*noun*)	coin	angolo	rincón
corridor 21	couloir	corridoio	pasillo
country 19	pays	paese	país
course 2 (*of a meal*)	plat/service	portata	plato
cover 14 (*noun*)	couvert	coprire	cubierto
cream 9	crème	panna	crema
credit card 25	carte de crédit	carta di credito	tarjeta de crédito
crispy 17	croustillant	croccante	crujiente
croissant 16	croissant	brioche	croissant
cube 14	cube	cubetto	cubito
curdle 17	cailler	coagularsi	cuajarse
currency 20	devise	valuta	divisa
curtain 21	rideau	tenda	cortina
daily 16	quotidien	ogni giorno	diario
dash 7 (*noun*)	goutte	goccio	pizca
date of birth 5	date de naissance	data di nascita	fecha de nacimiento
daughter 27	fille	figlia	hija
decorate 7	décorer	decorare	decorar
deep frier 16 (**US**: deep fryer)	friteuse	friggitrice	freidora
department store 22	grand magasin	grande magazzino	almacén
departure 27	départ	partenza	salida
deposit 26 (*noun*)	acompte	acconto	depósito
dessert 11	dessert	dessert	postre
dice 17 (*verb*)	couper en cubes	tagliare a dadi	cortar a dados
diner 26 (*noun*)	dîneur	cliente (di un ristorante)	cliente (de un restaurante)
dinner-jacket 20	smoking	smoking	smoking
direct 22 (*verb*)	indiquer le chemin	indicare la strada	indicar el camino
dirty 13	sale	sporco	sucio
dish 15 (*course*)	plat	piatto	plato
dishwasher 16	lave-vaisselle	lavastoviglie	lava-vajillas
district 10	région	regione	distrito
dizzy 23	pris d'étourdissement	preso da vertigini	mareado

WORD LIST

ENGLISH AND AMERICAN ENGLISH	GERMAN	GREEK
claret 10	roter Bordeaux	κόκκινο κρασί
clarified butter 17	geklärte Butter	στραγγισμένο βούτυρο (που έχει αφαιρεθεί το νερό)
clean 20 (*verb*)	reinigen	καθαρίζω
close 3 (*verb*)	schließen	κλείνω
clothes 20	Kleidung	ενδύματα
coat 5	Mantel	παλτό
cocktail 7	Cocktail	κοκτέϊλ
cocktail shaker 7	Cocktail Shaker	σέϊκερ για κοκτέϊλ
cod 9	Kabeljau	μπακαλιάρος
coffee shop 2	Cafe	καφετερία
colander 16	Durchschlag	τρυπητό
cold store 16	Kühlraum	θάλαμος ψύξης
college 27	College	κολλέγιο
comfortable 23	bequem	άνετος
commis 16 (**US**: junior)	Commis	(νεαρός) βοηθός του σέφ
company 26	Gesellschaft	εταιρία
complain 15	sich beschweren	παραπονούμαι
computer 18	Computer	ηλεκτρονικός υπολογιστής
conference 21	Konferenz	συνέδριο
confused 26	verwechselt	μπέρδεψε
cooked 9	gebraten	μαγειρευτό
copy 28 (*noun*)	Kopie	αντίγραφο
corkscrew 11	Korkenzieher	ανοιχτήρι μπουκαλιών
corner 26 (*noun*)	Ecke	γωνία
corridor 21	Gang	διάδρομος
country 19	Land	χώρα
course 2 (*of a meal*)	Gang	πιάτο (π.χ. πρώτο πιάτο)
cover 14 (*noun*)	decken	σερβίτσιο
cream 9	Sahne	κρέμα
credit card 25	Kreditkarte	πιστωτική κάρτα
crispy 17	kraus	τραγανιστός
croissant 16	Hörnchen	κρουασάν
cube 14	Würfel	κύβος
curdle 17	gerinnen	κόβω (π.χ. για μαγιονέζα)
currency 20	Währung	νομισματική μονάδα χώρας
curtain 21	Vorhang	κουρτίνα
daily 16	täglich	καθημερινά
dash 7 (*noun*)	Spritzer	λίγο/μια σταλιά (για συνταγές ποτών)
date of birth 5	Geburtsdatum	ημερομηνία γέννησις
daughter 27	Tochter	κόρη
decorate 7	verzieren	γαρνίρω/στολίζω
deep frier 16 (**US**: deep fryer)	Friteuse	φριτιέρα
department store 22	Kaufhaus	πολυκατάστημα
departure 27	Abflug	αναχώρηση
deposit 26 (*noun*)	Anzahlung	προκαταβολή
dessert 11	Dessert	επιδόρπιο
dice 17 (*verb*)	würfeln	κόβω σε κύβους
diner 26 (*noun*)	Speisegast	πελάτης εστιατορίου
dinner-jacket 20	Smokingjacke	σακκάκι για επίσημα γεύματα
direct 22 (*verb*)	den Weg zeigen	καθοδηγώ/δείχνω το δρόμο
dirty 13	schmutzig	βρώμικος
dish 15 (*course*)	Gericht	φαγητό
dishwasher 16	Geschirrspülmaschine	πλυντήριο πιάτων
district 10	Gegend	περιοχή
dizzy 23	schwindelig	ζαλισμένος

WORD LIST

ENGLISH AND AMERICAN ENGLISH	FRENCH	ITALIAN	SPANISH
do 3	faire	fare	hacer
double 1	double	doppio	doble
downstairs 21	en bas	al piano di sotto	abajo
drain 17 (*verb*)	égoutter	scolare	desagüe
draught 6 (**US**: on tap)	à la pression	alla spina	a presión
draughty 15 (**US**: drafty)	plein de courants d'air	esposto a correnti d'aria	con corrientes de aire
dressing 9 (*for salad*)	assaisonnement	condimento	aliño
dressing 23 (*for wounds*)	pansement (blessures)	medicazione	venda
dressing-table 21	coiffeuse	toilette (il mobile)	tocador
drinks 6 (*pl. noun*)	boissons	bevande	bebidas
dry 6 (*for wine*)	sec	secco	seco
duckling 9	caneton	anatroccolo	patito
early 18	de bonne heure	in anticipo	pronto
education 28	études/enseignement	istruzione	educación
egg 14	oeuf	uovo	huevo
egg yolk 17	jaune d'oeuf	tuorlo	yema
emergency 23	cas d'urgence	emergenza	caso de urgencia
employer 28	employeur	datore di lavoro	jefe
empty 13 (*adj.*)	vide	vuoto	vacío
enclose 28	inclure	allegare	incluir
enjoy 11	apprécier	gustare	disfrutar
enquire 28 (**US**: inquire)	se renseigner	richiedere informazioni	preguntar
equipment 16	ustensiles (de cuisine)	attrezzatura	equipamiento
escalope 9 (**US**: scallop)	escalope	scaloppina	escalope
every day 3	tous les jours	ogni giorno	todos los días
excellent 9	excellent	eccellente	excelente
exchange bureau 2 (**US**: currency exchange)	bureau de change	cambio	cambio
exhibition 23	exposition	mostra	exposición
exhibit 23 (*noun*)	objet exposé	oggetto esposto	objeto expuesto
exit 2	sortie	uscita	salida
expensive 10	cher	costoso	caro
experience 28	expérience	esperienza	experiencia
extra 8	en supplément	in più	extra
facilities 20	éléments de confort	attrezzature	facilidades
facing 21	en face de	di fronte a	frente a
family 27	famille	famiglia	familia
famous 10	célèbre	famoso	famoso
fall 23 (*verb*)	tomber	cadere	caer
far 22	loin	lontano	lejos
fat 10	graisse	grasso	grasa
fill 7	remplir	riempire	llenar
fill in 5 (*a form* **US**: fill out)	remplir (formulaire)	compilare	llenar
fillet 9	filet	filetto	filete
finally 7	pour terminer	per ultimo	por fin
find 11	trouver	trovare	encontrar
finely 17	finement	fine	finamente
fire 20	feu	incendio	fuego
fish 9 (*noun*)	poisson	pesce	pescado
fix 23	réparer	aggiustare	arreglar
flan 16	tarte	torta di frutta	pastel
flat 15 (*of beer*)	éventé	stantio	desventado
floor 5	étage	piano	piso
flour 14	farine	farina	harina

WORD LIST

ENGLISH AND AMERICAN ENGLISH	GERMAN	GREEK
do 3	tun/machen	κάνω
double 1	doppelt	διπλό
downstairs 21	unten	κάτω/στο κάτω πάτωμα
drain 17 (*verb*)	abgießen	στραγγίζω
draught 6 (**US**: on tap)	vom Faß	βαρελίσια (μπύρα)
draughty 15 (**US**: drafty)	zugig	εκτεθειμένος σε ρεύματα
dressing 9 (*for salad*)	Soße	σάλτσα σαλάτας (π.χ. Λαδόξυδο)
dressing 23 (*for wounds*)	Verband	επίδεσμος
dressing-table 21	Frisierkommode	κομοδίνο
drinks 6 (*pl. noun*)	Getränke	ποτά
dry 6 (*for wine*)	trocken	ξηρό
duckling 9	Entenküken	παπάκι

early 18	früh	νωρίς
education 28	Ausbildung	σπουδές
egg 14	Ei	αυγό
egg yolk 17	Eigelb	κρόκος
emergency 23	Notfall	επείγον περιστατικό
employer 28	Arbeitgeber	εργοδότης
empty 13 (*adj.*)	leer	κενός
enclose 28	beifügen	εσωκλείω
enjoy 11	genießen	απολαμβάνω
enquire 28 (**US**: inquire)	sich erkundigen	ζητώ πληροφορίες
equipment 16	Küchengeräte	εξοπλισμός
escalope 9 (**US**: scallop)	Schnitzel	εσκαλόπ
every day 3	jeden Tag	κάθε μέρα
excellent 9	ausgezeichnet	εξαιρετικός
exchange bureau 2	Wechselstube	υπηρεσία/γραφείο
(**US**: currency exchange)		συναλλάγματος
exhibition 23	Ausstellung	έκθεση
exhibit 23 (*noun*)	Ausstellungsstück	έκθεμα
exit 2	Ausgang	έξοδος
expensive 10	teuer	ακριβός
experience 28	Erfahrung	πείρα
extra 8	zusätzlich	εξτρά/επι πλέον

facilities 20	Einrichtungen	εξοπλισμός/προσφερόμενες υπηρεσίες
facing 21	gegenüber	απέναντι
family 27	Familie	οικογένεια
famous 10	berühmt	ξακουστός
fall 23 (*verb*)	fallen	πέφτω
far 22	weit	μακρυά
fat 10	dick	παχύς
fill 7	füllen	γεμίζω
fill in 5 (*a form* **US**: fill out)	ausfüllen	συμπληρώνω
fillet 9	Filet	φιλέτο
finally 7	zum Schluß	τελικά
find 11	finden	βρίσκω
finely 17	fein	σε μικρά/λεπτά κομμάτια
fire 20	Feuer	φωτιά
fish 9 (*noun*)	Fisch	ψάρι
fix 24	befestigen/in Ordnung bringen	φτιάχνω
flan 16	Kuchen	τάρτα
flat 15 (*of beer*)	schal	ξεθυμασμένη (για μπύρα)
floor 5	Stock	όροφος
flour 14	Mehl	αλεύρι

WORD LIST

ENGLISH AND AMERICAN ENGLISH	FRENCH	ITALIAN	SPANISH
flower shop 21 (US: florist)	fleuriste	fiorista	floristeria
fly 27 (verb)	prendre l'avion	volare	volar
folded 13	plié	piegato	plegado
food 8	nourriture	cibo	comida
foreign 20	étranger	estero	extranjero
forget 27	oublier	dimenticare	olvidar
fork 13	fourchette	forchetta	tenedor
foyer 21	hall	atrio	vestíbulo
French fries (US) 9 (UK: chips)	pommes frites	patate fritte	patatas fritas
fresh 11	frais	fresco	fresco
fridge 21	frigo	frigo	frigorífico
fruit 11	fruit	frutta	fruta
fruit salad 11	macédoine de fruits	macedonia	macedonia de fruta
fruity 12	fruité	profumato di frutta	afrutado
frying-pan 16	poêle	padella	sartén
full 1	complet	pieno	completo
full-bodied 10	qui a du corps	corposo	generoso (vino)
fully booked 4 (US: booked up)	complet	al completo	completo
further 22	plus loin	oltre	más lejos
garage 23	garage	garage	garage
garden 21	jardin	giardino	jardin
garlic 14	ail	aglio	ajo
garment 20	vêtement	indumento	vestido
gateau 11	gâteau	torta	torta
get 13	aller chercher	andare a prendere	conseguir
get up 3	se lever	alzarsi	levantarse
gift shop 21	boutique souvenirs	negozio di articoli regalo	tienda de regalos
gin 6	gin	gin	ginebra
glass 7	verre	bicchiere	vaso
glasses 23	lunettes	occhiali	gafas
go 3	aller	andare	ir
golf-course 21	terrain de golf	campo di golf	campo de golf
Greek 9	grec	greco	griego
green beans 9	haricots verts	fagiolini	judías verdes
grenadine 7	grenadine	grenadine	granadina
grilled 8	grillé	alla griglia	hecho a la parrilla
ground floor 21	rez-de-chaussée	pianterreno	planta baja
guest 5	client	ospite	huésped
gymnasium 21	salle de gymnastique	palestra	gimnasio
haircut 20	coupe de cheveux	taglio di capelli	corte de pelo
hairdressing 20	coiffure	parrucchiere	peinado
half 6 (pl. halves)	moitié	mezzo	mitad
halve 14 (verb)	couper en deux	tagliare in due	cortar en dos
hall porter 20	concierge, portier	portiere	conserje
ham 8	jambon	prosciutto	jamón
handicap facilities 2	installations pour handicapés	servizi per portatori di handicaps	facilidades para minus-válidos
handle 16	queue/manche	manico	mango
hanger 21	cintre	gruccia	percha
hard-boiled 9 (egg)	dur	sodo	huevo duro
head waiter 3	maître d'hôtel	capo cameriere	metre
health 23	santé	salute	salud

WORD LIST

ENGLISH AND AMERICAN ENGLISH	GERMAN	GREEK
flower shop 21 (**US**: florist)	Blumengeschäft	ανθοπωλείο
fly 27 (*verb*)	fliegen	πετάω/ταξιδεύω αεροπορικώς
folded 13	gefaltet	διπλωμένος
food 8	Essen	τροφή/φαγητό
foreign 20	ausländisch	ξένος/αλλοδαπός
forget 27	vergessen	ξεχνώ
fork 13	Gabel	πηρούνι
foyer 21	Eingangshalle	φουαγιέ
French fries (**US**) 9 (**UK**: chips)	Pommes frites	πατάτες τηγανιτές
fresh 11	frisch	φρέσκος
fridge 21	Kühlschrank	ψυγείο
fruit 11	Obst	φρούτα
fruit salad 11	Obstsalat	φρουτοσαλάτα
fruity 12	fruchtig	με γεύση απο σταφύλι
frying-pan 16	Bratpfanne	τηγάνι
full 1	voll	γεμάτος
full-bodied 10	vollmundig	δυνατό; (για κρασί; ευφημισμός)
fully booked 4 (**US**: booked up)	ausgebucht	εντελώς γεμάτο (για ξενοδοχείο/εστιατόριο)
further 22	weiter	πιό μακρυά
garage 23	Werkstatt	γκαράζ
garden 21	Garten	κήπος
garlic 14	Knoblauch	σκόρδο
garment 20	Kleidungsstück	ένδυμα
gateau 11	Torte	τούρτα
get 13	holen	φέρνω
get up 13	aufstehen	σηκώνομαι (το πρωί)
gift shop 21	Geschenkartikelgeschäft	κατάστημα δώρων
gin 6	Gin	τζίν
glass 7	Glas	ποτήρι
glasses 23	Brille	ποτήρια
go 3	gehen	πηγαίνω
golf-course 21	Golfplatz	γήπεδο γκόλφ
Greek 9	griechisch	Ελληνικός
green beans 9	grüne Bohnen	φασολάκια φρέσκα
grenadine 7	Grenadine	γκρεναντίνη
grilled 8	gegrillt	στη σχάρα
ground floor 21	Erdgeschoß	ισόγειο
guest 5	Gast	πελάτης/ένοικος ξενοδοχείου
gymnasium 21	Sportraum	γυμναστήριο
haircut 20	Haarschnitt	κούρεμα
hairdressing 20	Frisier-	κομμωτήριο
half 6 (*pl. halves*)	klein (Getränke)	μικρή/μικρές (για μπύρα)
halve 14 (*verb*)	halbieren	κόβω στα δυο
hall porter 20	Portier	θυρωρός
ham 8	Schinken	ζαμπόν
handicap facilities 2	Einrichtungen für Behinderte	εξυπηρέτηση ατόμων με αναπηρία
handle 16	Griff/Stiel	χερούλι
hanger 21	Kleiderbügel	κρεμάστρα
hard-boiled 9 (egg)	hartgekocht	σφιχτό (αυγό)
head waiter 3	Oberkellner	μαίτρ
health 23	Gesundheit	υγεία

ENGLISH AND AMERICAN ENGLISH	FRENCH	ITALIAN	SPANISH
heat lamp 16	lampe chauffante	lampada che mantiene caldo il cibo	lámpara infrarroja
high-class 28 (*adj.*)	de première classe	di prima categoria	de primera clase
hire 20	louer	noleggiare	alquilar
hob 16	plaque chauffante	piastra	plancha
hold 19 (*verb*)	tenir	tenere	tener
hole 16	trou	buco	agujero
hope 27 (*verb*)	espérer	sperare	esperar
horse-riding 21	équitation	equitazione	equitación
housekeeper 20	gouvernante	governante	ama de llaves
ice 6	glace	ghiaccio	hielo
ice-cream 12	glace (à manger)	gelato	helado
identification 25 (**US**: ID)	pièce d'identité	identificazione	identificación
immediately 15	tout de suite	subito	inmediatamente
include 25	comprendre/inclure	comprendere	incluir
indoor 21	d'intérieur	all'interno	cubierto
information 2	renseignements	informazioni	información
ingredients 7	ingrédients	ingredienti	ingredientes
inside 22	à l'intérieur	dentro	dentro
interview 28 (*noun*)	entrevue	colloquio	entrevista
invite 28	inviter	invitare	invitar
item 14	numéro/article	voce	pieza
jacket potato 9	pomme de terre en robe des champs	patata con la buccia (al forno)	patata sin pelar al horno
jewellery 20 (**US**: jewelry)	bijouterie	gioielli	joyería
job 27	travail	lavoro	trabajo
joint 13 (**US**: roast)	rôti	arrosto	asado
journey 27	voyage	viaggio	viaje
juicy 12	juteux	succoso	jugoso
julienne 17	julienne	tagliare a bastoncini	juliana
keep 16 (*verb*)	garder	tenere	guardar
key 5	clé	chiave	llave
key card 5	fiche d'hôtel	carta di accesso ai servizi	ficha del hotel
kidney 14	rognon	rognone	riñón
kitchen 16	cuisine	cucina	cocina
knead 17	pétrir	impastare	amasar
knife 13 (*pl. knives*)	couteau	coltello	cuchillo
ladle 16	louche	mestolo	cucharón
lager 6	bière blonde	birra bionda	cerveza rubia
lamb 9	agneau	agnello	cordero
lamp 16	lampe	lampada	lámpara
large 6	grand	grande	grande
late 18	en retard	in ritardo	con retraso
laundry 20	blanchissage	lavanderia	lavandería
layout 26	disposition	impaginazione	diseño
leave 3	quitter	partire	marcharse
left 13	gauche	sinistra	izquierda
leg 23	jambe	gamba	pierna
lemon 6	citron	limone	limón
letter 19	lettre	lettera	carta
lift 15 (**US**: elevator)	ascenseur	ascensore	ascensor

WORD LIST

ENGLISH AND AMERICAN ENGLISH	GERMAN	GREEK
heat lamp 16	Wärmelampe	θερμολαμπτήρας
high-class 28 (adj.)	erstklassig	πολυτελείας
hire 20	Verleih	νοικιάζω
hob 16	Kochmulde	εστία/μάτι κουζίνας
hold 19 (verb)	freihalten	κρατώ
hole 16	Loch	τρύπα
hope 27 (verb)	hoffen	ελπίζω
horse-riding 21	Reiten	ιππασία
housekeeper 20	Haushälterin	οικονόμος
ice 6	Eis	πάγος
ice-cream 12	Speiseeis	παγωτό
identification 25 (US: ID)	Ausweispapiere	ταυτότητα/διαβατήριο
immediately 15	sofort	αμέσως
include 25	einschließen	περιλαμβάνω
indoor 21	Hallen-	σκεπαστός (π.χ. πισίνα)
information 2	Informationen	πληροφορία/ες
ingredients 7	Zutaten	υλικά
inside 22	innen/drinnen	μέσα
interview 28 (noun)	Vorstellungsgespräch	συνέντευξη
invite 28	einladen	προσκαλώ
item 14	Posten	μέρος συνόλου η λίστας
jacket potato 9	Folienkartoffel	ψητή πατάτα ολόκληρη (με το φλούδι)
jewellery 20 (US: jewelry)	Schmuck	κοσμήματα
job 27	Stelle/Job	επάγγελμα
joint 13 (US: roast)	Braten	κομμάτι κρέατος
journey 27	Reise	ταξίδι
juicy 12	saftig	ζουμερός/χυμώδης
julienne 17	in feine Streifen schneiden	σε ψιλοκομμένες λωρίδες (για λαχανικά)
keep 16 (verb)	aufbewahren	διατηρώ
key 5	Schlüssel	κλειδί
key card 5	Schlüsselkarte	κλειδοκάρτα
kidney 14	Niere	νεφρό
kitchen 16	Küche	κουζίνα
knead 17	kneten	ζυμώνω
knife 13 (pl. knives)	Messer	μαχαίρι/α
ladle 16	Schöpfkelle	κουτάλα
lager 6	helles Bier	λάγκερ (εί δος μπύρας)
lamb 9	Lamm	αρνάκι γάλακτος
lamp 16	Lampe	πορτατίφ
large 6	groß	μεγάλος
late 18	spät	αργά
laundry 20	Wäscherei	πλυντήριο/πλύσιμο
layout 26	Plan	σχέδιο
leave 3	abfliegen/abreisen	αναχωρώ
left 13	links	αριστερός/ά
leg 23	Bein	γάμπα
lemon 6	Zitrone	λεμόνι
letter 19	Brief	γράμμα
lift 15 (US: elevator)	Fahrstuhl	ανελκυστήρας

ENGLISH AND AMERICAN ENGLISH	FRENCH	ITALIAN	SPANISH
light 10 (*adj.*)	léger	leggero	liviano/ligero
lime 7	citron vert/limette	limetta	lima
line 16 (*noun*)	ligne	catena	línea
lipstick 15	rouge à lèvres	rossetto	barra de labios
liqueur 11	liqueur	liquore	licor
liquid 7	liquide	liquido	líquido
lobby 21 (*noun*)	hall	atrio	recepción
lock 20 (*verb*)	fermer à clé	chiudere a chiave	cerrar con llave
long-necked 10	à long col	a collo lungo	cuellilargo
look like 27	ressembler à	sembrare	parecerse a
lost 27	perdu	perso	perdido
loud 18	bruyant	ad alta voce	ruidoso
luggage 5	bagages	bagagli	equipaje
lunch 3 (*noun*)	déjeuner	pranzo	almuerzo
maid 24 (*in hotel*)	femme de chambre	cameriera	camarera
mainly 28	surtout	principalmente	principalmente
make 7	faire	fare	hacer
manager 1	directeur	direttore	director
map 22	carte/plan	cartina	mapa
marital status 28	état civil	stato civile	estado civil
married 28	marié	sposato	casado
meal 2	repas	pasto	comida
measure 7 (*noun*)	mesure	misura	medida
medium 9 (*for steak*)	à point	medio	a punto
meeting 18	réunion/rendez-vous	riunione	reunión
melon 8	melon	melone	melón
melted 14	fondu	sciolto	derretida
menu 2	carte	menu	menú
men's toilet 2 (**US**: men's room)	toilettes pour messieurs	toilette per signori	servicio de caballeros
message 4	message	messaggio	mensaje
middle 13	milieu	centro	centro
milk 14	lait	latte	leche
milk shake 18	frappé	frappe	batido
mincer 16	hachoir	trita carne	picadora
missing 9	absent	mancante	que falta
mistake 26 (*noun*)	erreur	errore	error
mix 7	mélanger	mischiare	mezclar
modern 23	moderne	moderno	moderno
money 27	argent	soldi	dinero
museum 22	musée	museo	museo
mushroom 8	champignon	fungo	champiñón
name 1 (*noun*)	nom	nome	nombre
napkin 13	serviette	tovagliolo	servilleta
narrow 10	étroit	stretto	estrecho
nationality 19	nationalité	nazionalità	nacionalidad
near 22	près	vicino	cerca
never 7	jamais	mai	nunca
next 7	ensuite	poi	después
next door 20	à côté	alla porta accanto	al lado
night 1	nuit	notte	noche
noise 24	bruit	rumore	ruido
nothing 4	rien	niente	nada
notice 28 (*noun*)	préavis	preavviso	preaviso
number 1 (*noun*)	nombre	numero	número

Word List

ENGLISH AND AMERICAN ENGLISH	GERMAN	GREEK
light 10 (adj.)	leicht	ελαφρύς
lime 7	Limone	γλυκολέμονο
line 16 (noun)	Reihe	σειρά
lipstick 15	Lippenstift	κραγιόν
liqueur 11	Likör	λικέρ
liquid 7	Flüssigkeit	υγρός
lobby 21 (noun)	Halle	υποδοχή (ξενοδοχείου)
lock 20 (verb)	abschließen	κλειδώνω
long-necked 10	mit langem Hals	με μακρύ λαιμό
look like 27	aussehen wie	μοιάζω
lost 27	verloren	χαμένος
loud 18	laut	φωνασκών
luggage 5	Gepäck	αποσκευές
lunch 3 (noun)	Mittagstisch	μεσημεριανό γεύμα
maid 24 (in hotel)	Zimmermädchen	καμαριέρα
mainly 28	hauptsächlich	κυρίως
make 7	machen/zubereiten	φτειάχνω
manager 1	Geschäftsführer	διευθυντής
map	Stadtplan	χάρτης
marital status 28	Familienstand	έγγαμος κατάσταση
married 28	verheiratet	έγγαμος
meal 2	Mahlzeit	γεύμα
measure 7 (noun)	Maßeinheit	μεζούρα (για ποτά)
medium 9 (for steak)	halbdurch	μέτρια ψημμένο
meeting 18	Treffen	συνάντηση/συγκέντρωση
melon 8	Melone	πεπόνι
melted 14	zerlassen	λυωμένος
menu 2	Menü/Speisekarte	τιμοκατάλογος
men's toilet 2	Herrentoilette	ανδρική τουαλέτα
(US: men's room)		
message 4	Nachricht	μήνυμα
middle 13	Mitte	στο μέσον
milk 14	Milch	γάλα
milk shake 18	Milchmixgetränk	μιλκσέικ
mincer 16	Fleischwolf	κρεατομηχανή
missing 9	fehlend	λείπει
mistake 26 (noun)	Irrtum	λάθος
mix 7	mixen	φτειάχνω (ποτό κοκτέιλ)
modern 23	modern	μοντέρνος/σύγχρονος
money 27	Geld	χρήματα
museum 22	Museum	μουσείο
mushroom 8	Pilz/Champignon	μανιτάρι
name 1 (noun)	Name	όνομα
napkin 13	Serviette	πετσέτα φαγητού
narrow 10	schmal	στενός
nationality 19	Nationalität	εθνικότητα
near 22	in der Nähe	κοντά
never 7	nie	ποτέ
next 7	dann	ύστερα
next door 20	nebenan	δίπλα/στο διπλανό κτίριο
night 1	Nacht	βραδυά
noise 24	Lärm	θόρυβος
nothing 4	nichts	τίποτα
notice 28 (noun)	kündigen	προειδοποίηση (γιά παραίτηση)
number 1 (noun)	Nummer	αριθμός

ENGLISH AND AMERICAN ENGLISH	FRENCH	ITALIAN	SPANISH
obtain 20	obtenir	ottenere	obtener
obviously 24	évidemment	ovviamente	evidentemente
o'clock 3	(une) heure	l'ora	en punto
often 7	souvent	spesso	a menudo
olive 7	olive	oliva	aceituna
on call 20 (*e.g. night porter*)	de service	a disposizione	disponible
on foot 22 (**US**: walk)	à pied	a piedi	a pie
open 3	ouvert	aperto	abierto
opera 22	opéra	opera	ópera
opposite 21	en face	di fronte a	enfrente
order 8 (*verb*)	commander	ordinare	pedir
otherwise 20	autrement	altrimenti	de lo contrario
outdoor 21	en plein air	all'aperto	al aire libre
outside 22	à l'extérieur	fuori di	fuera
oven 16	four	forno	horno
overdone 15	trop cuit	troppo cotto	demasiado hecho
overtime 17	heures supplémentaires	straordinari	horas extras

ENGLISH AND AMERICAN ENGLISH	FRENCH	ITALIAN	SPANISH
package tour 26	voyage organisé	viaggio organizzato	viaje organizado
painkiller 23	calmant	analgesico	calmante
parasol 7	parasol	ombrellino	parasol
part-time 28	à mi-temps	a tempo parziale	por horas
pass through 7	passer	filtrare	pasar por
pastry 16	pâtisserie	pasta (per pasticceria)	pastelería
pay 25 (*verb*)	payer	pagare	pagar
peas 9	petits pois	piselli	guisantes
peel 17 (*verb*)	éplucher	sbucciare	pelar
per 2	par	per	por
permanent 23	permanent	permanente	permanente
petits fours 16	petits fours	pasticcini	pastelitos
phone call 20	appel téléphonique	telefonata	llamada telefónica
pie 9	en croûte	pasticcio	pastel
piece 11	morceau	pezzo	trozo
pint 6	pinte/en demi	pinta	pinta
plaice 9	plie/carrelet	passera di mare	platija
plan 23 (*verb*)	préparer/organiser	programmare	organizar
plate 13	assiette	piatto	plato
pleasant 27	agréable	piacevole	agradable
p.m. 3	du soir	di pomeriggio o di sera	por le tarde
poach 14	pocher	cuocere 'in camicia'	pasar por agua
popular 12	qui a du succès	popolare	popular
port 6	porto	porto	oporto
porter 5	portier	facchino	botones
portion 18	portion	porzione	porción
position 13	place	posizione	posición
post office 22	bureau de poste	ufficio postale	correos
poultry 16	volaille	pollame	aves
pour 7	verser	versare	verter
prawn 8	crevette	gamberetto	gamba
prefer 5	préférer	preferire	preferir
premises 16	lieux	in loco	local (es)
prepare 17	préparer	preparare	preparar
prescription 23	ordonnance	ricetta medica	receta
press 20 (*clothes*)	repasser	stirare	presionar
previous 28	précédent	precedente	anterior
profiteroles 11	profiteroles	profiteroles	profiteroles
purée 17	purée	purea	puré

WORD LIST

ENGLISH AND AMERICAN ENGLISH	GERMAN	GREEK
obtain 20	beziehen	αποκτώ
obviously 24	offensichtlich	προφανώς
o'clock 3	Uhr	η ώρα (π.χ. τρείς η ώρα)
often 7	oft	συχνά
olive 7	Olive	ελιά
on call 20 (*e.g. night porter*)	im Dienst	σε υπηρεσία
on foot 22 (**US**: walk)	on foot	με τα πόδια
open 3	geöffnet	ανοιχτός
opera 22	Oper	όπερα
opposite 21	gegenüber	απέναντι
order 8 (*verb*)	bestellen	παραγγέλνω
otherwise 20	sonst/anders	αλλοιώς
outdoor 21	im Freien	υπαίθριος
outside 22	draußen	έξω
oven 16	Backofen/Herd	φούρνος
overdone 15	verbraten	παραψημμένος
overtime 17	Überstunden	υπερωρία

package tour 26	Pauschalreise	ταξίδι 'πακέτο'
painkiller 23	Schmerzmittel	παυσίπονο
parasol 7	Sonnenschirm	διακοσμητική ομπρελλίτσα
part-time 28	Teilzeit-	μερική απασχόληση
pass through 7	durchpassieren/abgießen	περνώ απο (π.χ. σουρωτήρι)
pastry 16	Teig/Gebäck	γλυκίσματα
pay 25 (*verb*)	bezahlen	πληρώνω
peas 9	Erbsen	αρακάς
peel 17 (*verb*)	schälen	ξεφλουδίζω
per 2	pro	ανα/την (. . . ημέρα)
permanent 23	ständig	μόνιμος
petits fours 16	Petits fours	πτί φούρ
phone call 20	Telefongespräch	τηλεφώνημα
pie 9	Pastete	πίττα
piece 11	Stück	κομμάτι
pint 6	Pint (0,57 Liter)	μεγάλη μπύρα (περ. $\frac{1}{2}$ κιλό)
plaice 9	Scholle	είδος γλώσσας (ψάρι)
plan 23 (*verb*)	planen	σχέδιο
plate 13	Teller	πιάτο
pleasant 27	angenehm	ευχάριστος
p.m. 3	nachmittags/abends	μ.μ. (μετά μεσημβρίαν)
poach 14	dünsten/pochieren	ποσέ (π.χ. αυγά ποσέ)
popular 12	beliebt	δημοφιλής
port 6	Portwein	πορτό
porter 5	Portier	θυρωρός
portion 18	Portion	μερίδα
position 13	Platz	θέση
post office 22	Postamt	ταχυδρομείο
poultry 16	Geflügel	πουλερικά
pour 7	eingießen	ρίχνω (ποτό στο ποτήρι)
prawn 8	Garnele/Krabbe	γαρίδα
prefer 5	vorziehen	προτιμώ
premises 16	Haus	οίκημα/κτίριο
prepare 17	vorbereiten	προετοιμάζω
prescription 23	Rezept	ιατρική συνταγή
press 20 (*clothes*)	bügeln	σιδερώνω
previous 28	früher	προηγούμενος
profiteroles 11	Profiteroles	προφιτερόλ
purée 17	Püree	πουρές

WORD LIST

ENGLISH AND AMERICAN ENGLISH	FRENCH	ITALIAN	SPANISH
quarter 7	quart	quarto	cuarto
query 26 (*verb*)	demander une explication	mettere in dubbio	duda
quiet 18	tranquille	silenzioso	tranquilo
quite 12	assez	piuttosto	bastante
rack 16	égouttoir	scolapiatti	escurridor
ragout 17	ragoût	ragu	estofado
railway 22	chemin de fer	ferrovia	ferrocarril
rare 9 (*for steak*)	saignant	al sangúe	poco hecho
rarely 7	rarement	raramente	pocas veces
rate 26	taux/cours	tariffa	precio
ready 8	prêt	pronto	preparado
receipt 20	reçu	ricevuta	recibo
receptionist 5	réceptionniste	portiere d'albergo	recepcionista
red 10	rouge	rosso	rojo
refrigerator 16	frigidaire	frigorifero	refrigerador
registration card 5	fiche d'enregistrement	carta di registrazione	tarjeta de registro
relish 18 (*noun*)	assaisonnement	condimento	condimento
repair 20 (*verb*)	réparer	riparare	reparar
repeat 19	répéter	ripetere	repetir
replace 24	remplacer	sostituire	reponer
reserve 1	réserver	riservare	reservar
responsible 16	responsable	responsabile	responsable
restaurant diary 5 (**US**: reservation list)	livre des réservations	agenda di prenotazioni	libro de reservas
rice 9	riz	riso	arroz
right 13	droite	destra	derecha
right away 13	tout de suite	subito	en seguida
roast 14 (*noun*)	rôti	arrosto	asado
roll 16 (*noun*)	petit pain	panino	panecillo
rolled 14	enroulé	arrotolato	enrollado
roof 21	toit	tetto	tejado
room 3	chambre	camera	habitación
rough 12	rude	aspro	áspero
round 22 (*adv.* **US**: around)	autour	intorno	alrededor de
roundabout 22	rond-point	rondo	isla de tráfico
rum 6	rhum	rum	ron
rump steak 9	romsteck	bistecca di girello	solomillo
run 24 (*e.g. water*)	couler	scorrere	correr
safe 20 (*noun*)	coffre-fort	cassaforte	caja fuerte
salary 27	salaire	stipendio	sueldo
salmon 26	saumon	salmone	salmón
same day 20	le jour même	in giornata	el mismo día
sandwich 18	sandwich	tramezzino	bocadillo
sauce 9	sauce	salsa	salsa
saucepan 16	casserole	pentola	cazuela
sauna 2	sauna	sauna	sauna
sausage 18	saucisse	salsiccia	salchicha
sauté 17	sauté	far saltare in padella	saltear
scampi 9	langoustine	gamberi	gambas
seasoning 14	assaisonnement	condimento	condimento
see to 24 (*verb*)	veiller à ce que	far riparare	ocuparse de
serious 23	grave	serio	grave
serve 3	servir	servire	servir
settle 25 (~ *the bill*)	régler l'addition	saldare	ajustar
settle for 9	fixer son choix sur	decidere per	convenir en aceptar

WORD LIST

ENGLISH AND AMERICAN ENGLISH	GERMAN	GREEK
quarter 7	Viertel	τέταρτο
query 26 (*verb*)	reklamieren	θέτω ερώτημα
quiet 18	ruhig	χαμηλόφωνος
quite 12	ziemlich	αρκετά
rack 16	Gestell	υποδοχή/δίχτυ
ragout 17	Ragout	ραγού
railway 22	Eisenbahn	σιδηροδρομικός
rare 9 (*for steak*)	englisch	ψημμένος ελάχιστα
rarely 7	kaum	σπάνια
rate 26	Wechselkurs	τιμή
ready 8	bereit	έτοιμος
receipt 20	Quittung	απόδειξη
receptionist 5	Empfangschef/Empfangsdame	ρεσεψιονίστ
red 10	rot	κόκκινος
refrigerator 16	Kühlschrank	ψυγείο
registration card 5	Anmeldeformular	κάρτα πελάτου
relish 18 (*noun*)	Soße	ρέλις (πικάντικη σάλτσα με λαχανικά)
repair 20 (*verb*)	reparieren	επιδιορθώνω
repeat 19	wiederholen	επαναλαμβάνω
replace 24	austauschen	αντικαθιστώ
reserve 1	reservieren	κάνω κράτηση
responsible 16	verantwortlich	υπεύθυνος
restaurant diary 5 (**US**: reservation list)	Reservierungsplan	βιβλίο κρατήσεων εστιατορίου
rice 9	Reis	ρύζι
right 13	rechts	*1.* δεξιά, *2.* σωστός
right away 13	sofort	αμέσως
roast 14 (*noun*)	Braten	ψητό
roll 16 (*noun*)	Brötchen	ψωμάκι
rolled 14	gewendet	τυλιχτό
roof 21	Dach	ρούφ (γκάρντεν)
room 3	Raum	δωμάτιο
rough 12	herb	τραχύς
round 22 (*adv.* **US**: around)	um	γύρω απο
roundabout 22	Kreisverkehr	πλατεία (κυκλική)
rum 6	Rum	ρούμι
rump steak 9	Rumpsteak	στέικ απο κυλότο
run 24 (*e.g. water*)	fließen	τρέχω
safe 20 (*noun*)	Tresor	χρηματοκιβώτιο
salary 27	Gehalt	μισθός
salmon 26	Lachs	σολωμός
same-day 20	am selben Tag	αυθημερόν
sandwich 18	Sandwich	σάντουιτς
sauce 9	Sauce/Soße	σάλτσα
saucepan 16	Kochtopf	κατσαρόλα
sauna 2	Sauna	σάουνα
sausage 18	Wurst	λουκάνικο
sauté 17	sautieren	σωτάρω
scampi 9	Scampi	μεγάλες γαριδες
seasoning 14	Gewürz	αλατοπίπερο/καρύκευμα
see to 24 (*verb*)	sich kümmern um	φροντίζω
serious 23	ernst	σοβαρός
serve 3	servieren	σερβίρω
settle 25 (~ the bill)	begleichen	τακτοποιώ
settle for 9	sich entscheiden für	αποφασίζω

ENGLISH AND AMERICAN ENGLISH	FRENCH	ITALIAN	SPANISH
sew 20	coudre	cucire	coser
shake 7	secouer	sbattere	sacudir
shaker 7	shaker	shaker	coctelera
shape 10 (*noun*)	forme	forma	forma
sharpen 16	aiguiser	affilare	afilar
shave 20	(se) raser	radersi	afeitar (se)
shaver point 21 (**US:** shaver outlet)	prise rasoir	per il rasoio elettrico	enchufe para máquina de afeitar
sheet 24	drap	lenzuolo	sábana
shelf 21	rayon/étagère	ripiano	estante
sherry 6	sherry/xérès	sherry	jerez
shifts 16 (*work in ~*)	travailler en équipe de roulement	turni di lavoro	trabajar a turnos
shoemaker 23	cordonnier	calzolaio	zapatero
shop 20 (*noun*)	boutique/magasin	negozio	tienda
short-staffed 15	à court de personnel	a corto di personale	corto de personal
show 22 (*verb*)	montrer	indicare	enseñar
shower 21 (*noun*)	douche	doccia	ducha
side sal 9	salade d'accompagnement	contorno di insalata	ensalada (individual)
sieve 16	tamis/passoire	colino	tamiz
sign 25 (*verb*)	signer	firmare	firmar
signature 25	signature	firma	firma
single 1 (*~ room*)	simple	singolo	individual
sleep 24 (*verb*)	dormir	dormire	dormir
slice 7	tranche	fettina	cortada/loncha
small 6	petit	piccolo	pequeño
smoked 14	fumé	affumicato	ahumado
smooth 12 (*of wine*)	moelleux	velutato	liso
soap 24	savon	sapone	jabón
socket 21	prise	presa	enchufe
soda 6	soda (eau de Seltz)	acqua di selz	soda
soft-boiled 9 (*egg*)	à la coque	a la coque	blando
sole 9	sole	sogliola	lenguado
sometimes 7	quelquefois/parfois	qualche volta	a veces
soufflé 16	soufflé	souffle	soufflé
soup of the day 8	potage du jour	minestra del giorno	sopa del día
sour 9	aigre	acido	agrio
sparkling 10 (*wine*)	mousseux	frizzante	espumoso
speak up 19	parler plus fort	parlare a voce alta	hablar más alto
special 2	spécial	speciale	especial
spell 19 (*verb*)	épeler	scrivere lettera per lettera	deletrear
spend 27	dépenser	spendere	gastar
spicy 12	épicé/piquant	piccante	picante
spinach 9	épinards	spinaci	espinacas
spoon 13	cuiller	cucchiaio	cuchara
spot 14	endroit	luogo	lugar
sprinkle 17	arroser/saupoudrer	spargere	regar
squeezed 18	pressé	spremuto	exprimido
staff 9	personnel	personale	personal
stairs 21	escalier	scale	escalera
stale 15 (*of food*)	qui n'est pas frais	stantio	pasado
stamp 21 (*noun*)	timbre	francobollo	sello
stamp 25 (*verb*)	estampiller	timbrare	sellar
start 7	commencer	iniziare	empezar
starter 8 (**US:** appetizer)	entrée	antipasto	primer plato
stay 27 (*verb*)	rester	soggiornare	quedarse
steak 9	bifteck	bistecca	filete
stew 14 (*noun*)	ragoût	spezzatino	guiso
still 8 (*mineral water*)	non gazeuse	non gasato	no espumoso

ENGLISH AND AMERICAN ENGLISH	GERMAN	GREEK
sew 20	nähen	ράβω
shake 7	schütteln	ανακινώ
shaker 7	Shaker	σέϊκερ
shape 10 (*noun*)	Form	σχήμα
sharpen 16	schärfen	ακονίζω
shave 20	Rasur	ξύρισμα
shaver point 21 (**US**: shaver outlet)	Steckdose für Rasierapparate	πρίζα ξυριστικής μηχανής
sheet 24	Laken	σεντόνι
shelf 21	Regal	ράφι
sherry 6	Sherry	σέρρυ
shifts 16 (*work in* ∼)	Schicht	βάρδιες
shoemaker 23	Schuhmacher	υποδηματοποιός
shop 20 (*noun*)	Geschäft	κατάστημα
short-staffed 15	zu wenig Personal haben	με μειωμένο προσωπικό
show 22 (*verb*)	zeigen	δείχνω
shower 21 (*noun*)	Dusche	ντούς
side salad 9	Salat (als Beilage)	(μικρή)σαλάτα
sieve 16	Sieb	κόσκινο
sign 25 (*verb*)	unterschreiben	υπογράφω
signature 25	Unterschrift	υπογραφή
single 1 (*e.g.* ∼ *room*)	Einzel-	μονό (π.χ. δωμάτιο)
sleep 24	schlafen	κοιμάμαι
slice 7	Scheibe	φέτα
small 6	klein	μικρός
smoked 14	geräuchert	καπνιστό
smooth 12 (*of wine*)	lieblich	γλυκόπιοτο
soap 24	Seife	σαπούνι
socket 21	Steckdose	πρίζα
soda 6	Soda	σόδα
soft-boiled 9 (*egg*)	weichgekocht	μελάτο
sole 9	Seezunge	γλώσσα (ψάρι)
sometimes 7	manchmal	μερικές φορές
soufflé 16	Soufflé	σουφλέ
soup of the day 8	Tagessuppe	σούπα της ημέρας
sour 9	sauer	ξυνός
sparkling 10 (*wine*)	Schaum-	σαμπανιζέ
speak up 19	lauter sprechen	δυναμώνω τη φωνή
special 2	besonders	σπέσιαλ
spell 19	buchstabieren	λέω ή γράφω γράμματα λέξης
spend 27	ausgeben	ξοδεύω χρήματα
spicy 12	würzig	πικάντικος
spinach 9	Spinat	σπανάκι
spoon 13	Löffel	κουτάλι
spot 15	Platz	σημείο
sprinkle 17	sprenkeln	ραντίζω/πασπαλίζω
squeezed 18	gepreßt	στιμμένος
staff 9	Personal	προσωπικό
stairs 21	Treppe	σκάλες
stale 15 (*of food*)	schal/alt	μπαγιάτικος
stamp 21 (*noun*)	Briefmarke	γραμματόσημο
stamp 25 (*verb*)	stempeln	σφραγίζω
start 7	anfangen	αρχίζω
starter 8 (**US**: appetizer)	Vorspeise	πρώτο πιάτο
stay 27 (*verb*)	wohnen	μένω
steak 9	Steak	μπριζόλα
stew 14 (*noun*)	Eintopfgericht	εντράδα/κρέας κατσαρόλας με λαχανικά
still 8 (*mineral water*)	ohne Kohlensäure	χωρίς ανθρακικό

WORD LIST

ENGLISH AND AMERICAN ENGLISH	FRENCH	ITALIAN	SPANISH
stir 7 (*verb*)	remuer	rimescolare	remover
stockpot 16	marmite à bouillon	marmitta	puchero para el caldo
stool 21	tabouret	sgabello	taburete
straight ahead 22	tout droit	sempre dritto	todo recto
straight away 20 (**US**: right away)	tout de suite	subito	en seguida
strain 17 (*verb*)	passer	scolare	colar
strainer 7	passoire	colino	colador
strap 23 (*on sandal*)	courroie	cinturino	correa
street 2	rue	strada	calle
stuffed 8	farci	riempito	relleno
stuffing 14 (*for meat*)	farce	ripieno	relleno
subway 22	passage souterrain	sottopassaggio	pasaje subterráneo
sugar 24	sucre	zucchero	azúcar
sunny side up 9 (*for egg*)	oeuf sur le plat/au miroir	uovo all'occhio di bue	huevo al plato
supply 16 (*verb*)	fournir	fornire	abastecer
surname 28 (**US**: last name)	nom de famille	cognome	apellido
sweet 6 (*wine*)	doux	amabile	dulce
sweet 11 (**US**: dessert)	dessert	dolce	postre
swimming-pool 2	piscine	piscina	piscina
switch 17 (*noun*)	interrupteur	frustino	interruptor
T junction 22 (**US**: intersection)	intersection	incrocio	cruce (en forma de T.)
table 1	table	tavolo	mesa
table d'hôte 2	table d'hôte	a prezzo fisso	menú (del día)
take 7	prendre	prendere	coger
take off 14	supprimer	togliere	quitar
taste 15 (*verb*)	goûter	assaggiare	gustar
tasty 12	qui a du goût/relevé	saporito	sabroso
telephone call 26	appel téléphonique	telefonata	llamada telefónica
television (TV) 21	télévision	televisore	televisión
temperature 12	température	temperatura	temperatura
tender 12 (*of meat*)	tendre	tenero	tierno
theatre 20 (US: theater)	théâtre	teatro	teatro
thin 14	mince	sottile	fino
throw out 7	vider	buttare fuori	tirar
ticket 18	billet	biglietto	billete
time of year 23	saison	stagione	estación del año
toast 18 (*noun*)	toast	pane tostato	tostada
toilet 2	toilettes	toilette	lavabo
toilet paper 24	papier hygiénique	carta igienica	papel higiénico
tomato 9	tomate	pomodoro	tomate
tomorrow 4	demain	domani	mañana
tonic 6	tonique	tonico	tónica
tonight 4	ce soir	stasera	esta noche
too 12	aussi	anche	también
top 11	haut (en haut)	parte superiore	parte de arriba
topped with 9	avec . . . par dessus	coperto	con . . . encima
total 25	total	totale	total
touch 24 (*verb*)	toucher	toccare	tocar
tough 12 (*of meat*)	dur (viande)	duro	tirante
towel 24	serviette	asciugamano	toalla
town 10	ville	città	ciudad
traffic lights 22	feux de signalisation	semaforo	semáforos
train 22 (*noun*)	train	treno	tren
trained 18	qualifié	prepararsi professionalmente	formado
travel 3 (*verb*)	voyager	viaggiare	viajar

98

Word List

ENGLISH AND AMERICAN ENGLISH	GERMAN	GREEK
stir 7 (verb)	rühren	ανακατεύω
stockpot 16	Suppentopf	μεγάλη κατσαρόλα για βράση κρεάτων
stool 21	Hocker	σκαμπό
straight ahead 22	geradeaus	κατ᾽ευθείαν μπροστά
straight away 20 (US: right away)	sofort	αμέσως
strain 17 (verb)	abgießen	σουρώνω/περνώ απο τρυπητό
strainer 7	Sieb	σουρωτήρι
strap 23 (on sandal)	Riemen	λουρί
street 2	Straße	δρόμος
stuffed 8	gefüllt	γεμιστό
stuffing 14 (for meat)	Füllung	γέμιση
subway 22	Unterführung	υπόγειος σιδηρόδρομος
sugar 24	Zucker	ζάχαρη
sunny side up 9 (for egg)	mit heilem Dotter	μάτια (για αυγά)
supply 16 (verb)	liefern	προμηθεύω
surname 28 (US: last name)	Nachname	επώνυμο
sweet 6 (wine)	süß	γλυκό (κρασί)
sweet 11 (US: dessert)	Nachspeise	γλυκό (επιδόρπιο)
swimming-pool 2	Schwimmbad	πισίνα
switch 17 (noun)	Schalter	διακόπτης

T junction 22 (US: intersection)	Vorfahrtsstraße	διασταύρωση σχήματος Τ
table 1	Tisch	τραπέζι
table d'hôte 2	Table d'hôte	τάμπλ ντότ
take 7	nehmen	παίρνω
take off 14	streichen	αποσύρω
taste 15 (verb)	probieren	γεύομαι. δοκιμάζω
tasty 12	lecker	νόστιμος
telephone call 26	Telefongespräch	τηλεφώνημα
television (TV) 21	Fernsehen	τηλεόραση
temperature 12	Temperatur	θερμοκρασία
tender 12 (of meat)	zart	μαλακό/τρυφερό (κρέας)
theatre 20 (US: theater)	Theater	θέατρο
thin 14	dünn	λεπτός
throw out 7	ausschütten	πετώ
ticket 18	Karte	εισητήριο
time of year 23	Jahreszeit	εποχή του χρόνου
toast 18 (noun)	Toast	φρυγανισμένο φωμί
toilet 2	Toilette	τουαλέτα
toilet paper 24	Toilettenpapier	χαρτί υγειας
tomato 9	Tomate	τομάτα
tomorrow 4	morgen	αύριο
tonic 6	Tonic	τόνιχ
tonight 4	heute abend	απόψε
too 12	auch	επίσης
top 11	oberes Teil	στο πάνω μέρος
topped with 9	bedeckt	σκεπασμένο
total 25	Gesammtsumme	σύνολο
touch 24 (verb)	berühren	ακουμπώ, αγγίζω
tough 12 (of meat)	zäh	σκληρό (για κρέας)
towel 24	Handtuch	πετσέτα
town 10	Stadt	πόλη
traffic lights 22	Ampel	φανάρια τροχαίας
train 22 (noun)	Zug	τραίνο
trained 18	ausgebildet werden	εκπαιδευμένος
travel 3 (verb)	reisen	ταξιδεύω

WORD LIST

ENGLISH AND AMERICAN ENGLISH	FRENCH	ITALIAN	SPANISH
travel agency 18	agence de voyages	agenzia di viaggi	agencia de viajes
traveller's cheque 25	chèque de voyage	travellers cheque	cheques de viaje
tray 14	plateau	vassoio	bandeja
trimmings 14	garniture	decorazioni	guarnición
trip 27 (noun)	voyage	viaggio	viaje
trolley 11 (US: cart)	chariot	carrello	carrito
tuna 18	thon	tonno	atún
turbot 9	turbot	rombo	rodaballo
umbrella 23	parapluie	ombrello	paraguas
undercooked/underdone 15	pas assez cuit	poco cotto	poco hecho
underground 27 (US: subway)	métro	metropolitana	metro
underneath 11	en dessous	sotto	debajo
uneatable 15	immangeable	immangiabile	no se puede comer
unit 26	unité	scatto	unidad
unmade 24	pas fait/défait	disfatto	deshecho
until 19	jusqu'à	fino a	hasta
upstairs 21	en haut (de l'escalier)	al piano di sopra	arriba
usually	d'ordinaire	di solito	normalmente
utensils 16	ustensiles	utensili	utensilios
vacancy 28	poste vacant	posto libero	vacante
valuables 20	objets de valeur	oggetti di valore	objeto de valor
Value Added Tax (VAT) 25 (US: Sales Tax)	Taxe à la Valeur Ajoutée (TVA)	Imposta sul Valore Aggiunto (IVA)	Impuesto al Valor Añadido (IVA)
variety 16	variété/diversité	varietà	variedad
veal 9	veau	vitello	ternera
vegetable 9	légume	verdura	verdura
vegetarian 9	végétarien	vegetariano	vegetariano
vinegary 12 (of wine)	acide/qui a un goût de vinaigre	che sa di aceto	avinagrado
visit 23 (verb)	visiter	visitare	visitar
wardrobe 21	armoire	armadio	guardarropa
waste 27 (verb)	gaspiller	sprecare	desperdiciar
waste-paper basket 24	corbeille à papier	cestino per la carta straccia	papelera
water jug 13 (US: water pitcher)	pot à eau	brocca	jarra para el agua
wear 20 (verb)	porter (vêtements)/mettre	indossare	usar
well 23	bien	bene	de buena salud
wet 17 (adj.)	mouillé	bagnato	mojado
whisk 16 (noun)	fouet	frusta	batidor
whisky 6 (US: whiskey)	whisky	whisky	whisky
white 10	blanc	bianco	blanco
window 8	fenêtre	finestra	ventana
wine 6	vin	vino	vino
wine list 8	carte des vins	carta dei vini	carta de vinos
without 15	sans	senza	sin
women's toilet 2 (US: women's room)	toilettes pour dames	toilette per signore	servicio de señoras
wonderful 15	merveilleux	meraviglioso	maravilloso
wooden spoon 16	cuiller en bois	cucchiaio di legno	cuchara de madera
wound 23	blessure	ferita	herida
x-ray 23	rayons-X/radioscopie	raggi x	rayos x
zoo 22	zoo	zoo	jardín zoológico

ENGLISH AND AMERICAN ENGLISH	GERMAN	GREEK
travel agency 18	Reisebüro	γραφείο ταξιδίων
traveller's cheque 25	Reisescheck	ταξιδιωτική επιταγή
tray 14	Tablett	δίσκος
trimmings 14	Beilagen/Verzierungen	γαρνιτούρα
trip 27 (*noun*)	Reise	ταξίδι
trolley 11 (**US**: cart)	Servierwagen	τραπεζάκι με ρόδες
tuna 18	Thunfisch	τόννος (ψάρι)
turbot 9	Steinbutt	συάκι (ψάρι)
umbrella 23	Regenschirm	ομπρέλλα
undercooked/underdone 15	nicht gar	άψητο, όχι αρκετά ωημμένο
underground 27 (**US**: subway)	U-Bahn	υπόγειος σιδηρόδρομος
underneath 11	unter	από κάτω
uneatable 15	nicht eßbar	δέν τρώγεται
unit 26	Einheit	μονάδα (τηλεφωνικής συνδιάλεξης)
unmade 24	ungemacht	άφτειαχτο
until	bis	εως, μέχρι
upstairs 21	oben	επάνω, στό πάνω πάτωμα
usually	gewöhnlich	συνήθως
utensils 16	Utensilien	μαγειρικά σκεύη
vacancy 28	offene Stelle	κενή θέση (για δουλειά)
valuables 20	Wertsachen	τιμαλφή
Value Added Tax (VAT) 25 (**US**: Sales Tax)	Mehrwertsteuer	Φόρος Προστι θέμενης Αξίας (ΦΠΑ)
variety 16	Auswahl	ποικιλία
veal 9	Kalb	μοσχαράκι γάλακτος
vegetable 9	Gemüse	λαχανικό
vegetarian 9	vegetarisch	χορτοφάγος
vinegary 12 (*of wine*)	wie Essig	σάν ξύδι (για κρασί)
visit 23 (*verb*)	besuchen	επισκέπτομαι
wardrobe 21	Kleiderschrank	ντουλάπα
waste 27 (*verb*)	verschwenden	σπαταλώ
waste-paper basket 24	Papierkorb	καλάθι για άχρηστα
water jug 13 (**US**: water pitcher)	Wasserkaraffe	κανάτα νερού
wear 20 (*verb*)	tragen	φορώ
well 23	gut	καλά
wet 17 (*adj.*)	naß	υγρός
whisk 16 (*noun*)	Schneebesen/ Rührgeraät	χτυπητήρι (π.χ. για αυγά)
whisky 6 (**US**: whiskey)	Whisky	ουίσκυ
white 10	weiß	λευκός
window 8	Fenster	παράθυρο
wine 6	Wein	κρασί
wine list 8	Weinkarte	κατάλογος κρασιών
without 15	ohne	χωρίς
women's toilet 2 (**US**: women's room)	Damentoilette	γυναικεία τουαλέτα
wonderful 15	wunderbar	υπέροχος
wooden spoon 16	Holzlöffel	ξύλινη κουτάλα
wound 23	Wunde	τραύμα
x-ray 23	röntgen	ακτινογραφία
zoo 22	Zoo	ζωολογικός κήπος

APPENDIX 1 IRREGULAR VERBS

INFINITIVE	PAST TENSE	PAST PARTICIPLE	INFINITIVE	PAST TENSE	PAST PARTICIPLE
be	was	been	lend	lent	lent
beat	beat	beaten	let	let	let
become	became	become	lie	lay	lain
begin	began	begun	light	lit	lit
bend	bent	bent	lose	lost	lost
bite	bit	bitten	make	made	made
blow	blew	blown	mean	meant	meant
break	broke	broken	meet	met	met
bring	brought	brought	put	put	put
build	built	built	read	read	read
burn	burnt	burnt	ride	rode	ridden
buy	bought	bought	ring	rang	rung
catch	caught	caught	rise	rose	risen
choose	chose	chosen	run	ran	run
come	came	come	say	said	said
cost	cost	cost	see	saw	seen
cut	cut	cut	sell	sold	sold
dig	dug	dug	send	sent	sent
do	did	done	set	set	set
draw	drew	drawn	shake	shook	shaken
dream	dreamt	dreamt	shine	shone	shone
drink	drank	drunk	shoot	shot	shot
drive	drove	driven	shut	shut	shut
eat	ate	eaten	sing	sang	sung
fall	fell	fallen	sink	sank	sunk
feed	fed	fed	sit	sat	sat
feel	felt	felt	sleep	slept	slept
fight	fought	fought	slide	slid	slid
find	found	found	smell	smelt	smelt
fly	flew	flown	speak	spoke	spoken
forget	forgot	forgotten	spend	spent	spent
freeze	froze	frozen	stand	stood	stood
get	got	got	steal	stole	stolen
give	gave	given	stick	stuck	stuck
go	went	gone	strike	struck	struck
hang	hung	hung	swear	swore	sworn
have	had	had	swim	swam	swum
hear	heard	heard	take	took	taken
hide	hid	hidden	teach	taught	taught
hit	hit	hit	tear	tore	torn
hold	held	held	tell	told	told
hurt	hurt	hurt	think	thought	thought
keep	kept	kept	throw	threw	thrown
know	knew	known	understand	understood	understood
lay	laid	laid	wake	woke	woke/woken
lead	led	led	wear	wore	worn
lean	leant	leant	win	won	won
learn	learnt	learnt	write	wrote	written
leave	left	left			

APPENDIX 2 EXTRA WORD CATEGORIES

Extra Word categories with unit number:

aperitifs 8

bathroom equipment 21
bed equipment 24
bills 26

clothes 20
cocktails 7
cooking operations 17
countries/nationalities 10, 19
crockery 16
currencies 2, 25
customers' complaints 15
cutlery 13

the day 4
days of the week 1
directions 10

emergency services 23

family 27
fish 12
fractions 7
fruit 11

greetings 1
grilled meat 9

health care personnel 23
health problems 23
herbs 12
holidays 4
hot drinks 18
hotel activities 20, 21

kitchen equipment 17

letter abbreviations 28
liqueurs 7

meals 3
meat 9
methods of cooking 9
mixers 6
months 5

numbers 1, 2, 5

offal 14

payment terms 25
personal details 28
poultry 13

restaurant staff 3
road signs 22
room equipment 24
room types 1

seasons 3
service 26
shellfish 14
smokers' equipment 13
snacks 18
spices 12
spirits 6
starters 8
stationery 24
street terms 22

telephone terms 19
titles 3
transport 22

vegetables 9

wines (fortified) 6
wines (table) 6
wine terms 10

the year 4

APPENDIX 3 ROLE PLAY INFORMATION

A

Name	Sarah Lee
Address	4 Victor Street York England
Date of Birth	12.4.68
Passport No.	L 784789 C
Issued at	Liverpool
Date of issue	31.3.87
Next address	Home

2 useful standard codes for clarifying spellings over the telephone:

A	Alpha		**A**	Andrew
B	Bravo		**B**	Benjamin
C	Charlie		**C**	Charlie
D	Delta		**D**	David
E	Echo		**E**	Edward
F	Foxtrot		**F**	Frederick
G	Glove		**G**	George
H	Hotel		**H**	Harry
I	India		**I**	Isaac
J	Juliet		**J**	Jack
K	Kilo		**K**	King
L	Lima		**L**	Lucy
M	Mike		**M**	Mary
N	November		**N**	Nellie
O	Oscar		**O**	Oliver
P	Papa		**P**	Peter
Q	Quebec		**Q**	Queenie
R	Romeo		**R**	Robert
S	Sierra		**S**	Sugar
T	Tango		**T**	Tommy
U	Uniform		**U**	Uncle
V	Victor		**V**	Victor
W	William		**W**	William
X	X-ray		**X**	Xmas
Y	Yankie		**Y**	Yellow
Z	Zulu		**Z**	Zebra

APPENDIX 3 ROLE PLAY INFORMATION

B

Name	Wim Van de Veen
Address	Haarlemstraat 19 Utrecht The Netherlands
Date of Birth	17.11.62
Passport No.	F 7304722
Date of issue	14.2.88
Next address	Randolph Hotel Oxford, UK

Unit 1

Listening one 1 Good afternoon 2 I'd like to 3 Could I 4 Please? 5 can I have 6 One moment,

Practice 1 Good afternoon, can I help you? 2 I'd like to book a double room for 4 nights. 3 I'd like to reserve a table for 5 for Tuesday. 4 Yes madam, what name please? 5 Could I speak to the manager, please? 6 I'd like to book a single room from Monday to Thursday. 7 Yes sir, who's calling please? 8 I'd like to reserve a table for two for Saturday at 8 pm.

Listening two 4, 7, 8, 6, 5, 2, 9, 3, 1, 10

Activity *Across:* 1 NIGHTS 4 MORNING 5 RESERVE 8 DOUBLE 10 NO *Down:* 1 NAME 2 SINGLE 3 TUESDAY 6 EVENING 7 MONDAY 9 BOOK

Unit 2

Listening one a £55 b 16 c £11.50

Practice 1 'm 2 's 3 's 4 are 5 There's 6 are

Listening two 1 The charge for a single room: 850 F per night 2 A children's menu: £5 3 A beer: $1.25 4 The charge for a double room: £65 per night 5 the cost of the table d'hôte menu: £16.50.

Unit 3

Listening one 1 12.00 2 2.30 3 Mondays (in winter) 4 Sunday 5 six 6 1 pm 7 Mrs Richards
(Using the 12 hour clock, 12 midnight to 12 midday is am; 12 midday to 12 midnight is pm.
Note: 12 am = midnight   12 pm = midday)

Practice 1 Are you open every day? We're closed on Mondays. 2 What time do you serve dinner? We serve dinner from 7 to 11. 3 Do you have a table for 6 for Saturday lunch? Yes madam, for what time? 4 What time do you open in the evening? We open at 7 o'clock. 5 Do you have a single room for Friday? Certainly. What name is it please?

Listening two 1 7.45 2 10.00 3 6.45/18.45 4 2.05/14.05 5 12.30 6 8.25/20.25

Activity These example sentences may help students to avoid mistakes:
In the evening I watch TV. **At** night I go to sleep. **In** winter we go ski-ing, usually **at** Christmas. I leave home **at** 7.30. I go home **at** 4 o'clock. I stay **at** home **on** Sundays. I go to college **by** bus.

Unit 4

Listening one 2 how many – for two 3 When? – for Sunday lunch 4 What? – a family room 5 When? – for tonight 6 Who? – Mr Yossarian. Where? – in room 101

Practice 1 We're open six days per week. 2 We don't open on Mondays. 3 I'm afraid we don't have any rooms tonight. 4 I'm sorry he isn't here/he's not here. 5 I'm afraid we haven't any tables left for Friday night. 6 It's a very busy night. 7 We don't serve lunch before 12 o'clock. 8 They haven't left a message. 9 They're open every evening. 10 She doesn't have lunch at home.

Listening two 70 dollars; Wednesday; 2.15; 90 francs; Tuesday at 5.25; 18 marks; Saturday am; £60; 10.30

Activity These are model answers. Students' answers may be different but correct.
1 Q. What time does the bar open? A. It opens at 6 o'clock. It closes at midnight.
2 Q. Can we have a table for two, please? A. I'm afraid we're fully booked tonight.
3 Q. Hello, can I speak to Mr. Black in room 109, please? A. I'm sorry but there's no answer. Can I take a message?
4 Q. Good morning, can I reserve a table for six for tomorrow at 8.30 please? A. Certainly, madam. What name is it, please?

Unit 5

Listening one 1 receptionist 2 guest 3 registration card 4 key card 5 key 6 room number 7 luggage 8 porter 9 waiter 10 table for 3 11 restaurant bookings diary 12 coats

Practice A 1 his 2 their 3 our 4 her 5 my
B 2 Would you like to put your car in the car park?
3 Would you like/prefer to have breakfast in your room?
4 Would you like to leave your coat? 5 Would you like to leave a message for your friend?

Listening two Note: when speaking dates we say April *the* eleventh, or *the* eleventh *of* April. Sometimes people do not use *the*, *'th* and *of* in writing dates; they write 11 April, 1 May, 5 June etc.
1 April 11th/11th April 2 Saturday 3 (the) 29th 4 No, it's a Monday. 5 Sunday 6 (the) 7th 7 Yes. 8 (the) 5th 9 Saturday.

Unit 6

Listening one Tim – a pint of beer. Denise – a gin and tonic. Michael – a pint of lager. Jill – a dry sherry.

Practice Model answers. 1 Could I have a sherry, please? Would you like sweet or dry, madam? 2 Can I have a beer, please? Would you like a pint or a half, sir? 3 Could I have a glass of port? Would you like a small or a large one, sir? 4 A whisky, please. Certainly sir. Would you like water or soda? 5 Could I have a lager? Yes madam, would you like draught or bottled?

Listening two 1 £2.90 2 £1.00 3 £2.40 4 £3.22 5 £3.30

Activity brandy, cognac, coke, gin, martini, rum, vodka, water, whisky, wine.

ANSWER KEY

Unit 7

Listening one g, j, a, i, e, l, f, h, d, c, k, b.

Listening two Daiquiri ingredients: broken ice, lime juice, rum, grenadine
Manhattan ingredients: ice, Canadian Club whisky, Italian vermouth, Angostura bitters
(Check the tapescript for method).

Activity 5, 2, 7, 3, 1, 4, 6

Unit 8

Listening one 1 menus and wine list 2 Campari and soda 3 medium dry sherry 4 cream of mushroom 5 no 6 mixed hors d'oeuvres 7 bread

Practice 1 the, the 2 an 3 the 4 a 5 a 6 the

Listening two 1 1 grilled sardines and 1 avocado pear with prawns 2 2 melon with Parma ham and 1 bottle of still mineral water 3 1 pâté 4 1 mixed hors d'oeuvres

Activity 1 some wine/a glass of wine 2 some bread 3 a table by the window 4 some mineral water 5 an aperitif 6 some salt 7 some wine 8 some soup 9 the wine list 10 some ice

Unit 9

Listening one 1 turbot, duchesse potatoes and spinach 2 medium rare rump steak, jacket potato, mushrooms and side salad

Practice **A** 1 How would you like your egg madam, hard or soft-boiled? I'd like it hard, please.
2 How would you like your jacket potato sir, with butter or sour cream? I'd like it with butter, please.
3 How would you like your egg, turned over or sunny side up? I'd like it sunny side up, please.
4 How would you like your coffee, black or white? I'd like it black, please. 5 How would you like your salad, with French dressing or mayonnaise? I'd like it with French dressing, please.
B 1 any 2 some 3 any 4 any 5 some (polite form question) 6 any
C 1 I'm afraid we haven't any fillet steak but the rump's very good. 2 I'm afraid we haven't any pâté de foie gras, but the pâté de canard is excellent.
3 I'm afraid we haven't any cod but the plaice is very good.

Listening two Table 17: 1 scampi and duckling, spinach, green beans and a side salad. Table 16: 1 fillet steak rare, side salad, French fries. Table 11: 1 veal escalope, 1 turbot, green beans, jacket potato.

Unit 10

Listening one Chablis, Liebfraumilch, Muscadet, Beaujolais, Beaune, Bergerac.
The guests choose the Chablis and the Bergerac.

Practice 1 Riesling is sweeter than Graves. 2 A Burgundy bottle is fatter than a Bordeaux bottle. 3 Rosé is not as full-bodied as claret. 5 A Riesling bottle is narrower than a Burgundy bottle. 6 Mineral water is cheaper than table wine. 7 Beaujolais is not as expensive as champagne.

Listening two 1 Dão 2 Port 3 Sherry 4 Rioja 5 Champagne 6 Loire valley: Muscadet, Sancerre 7 Bordeaux: Médoc, St. Emilion, Graves 8 Burgundy: Beaujolais, Mâcon 9 Chianti 10 Frascati

Activity *Across:* 1 COCKTAIL SHAKER 4 VERMOUTH 8 ICE 10 AVOCADO 12 KIR 13 WINE 16 NORTH 17 RADISH 18 PORT 19 INTO
Down: 1 CAULIFLOWER 2 APERITIF 3 RICE 5 OLIVE 6 TO 7 VEAL 9 PORK 11 CHIANTI 14 AS 15 HOT

Unit 11

Listening one 1 apple pie 2 chocolate gâteau 3 Charlotte Russe 4 fresh fruit salad 5 profiteroles 6 blackcurrant cheese cake 7 fresh fruit basket 8 English Cheddar 9 Stilton 10 Camembert 11 Dolce Latte

Practice **A** 1 Would you like to order now, madam? (a).
2 Do you want coffee, Bella? (c). 3 Could I have your name, please? (a). 4 Can I get you some more drinks? (b).
5 Would you like sparkling or still, madam? (a). 6 May I suggest the Graves, sir? (a).
B 1 on 2 with 3 in, on 4 with 5 in

Listening two The three types of cheese are hard, soft and blue. Hard: Britain – Cheddar; Netherlands – Edam; Switzerland – Gruyère; Spain – Manchego; Italy – Parmesan. Soft: France – Camembert and Brie. Blue: Britain – Stilton; France – Roquefort; Italy – Gorgonzola; Denmark – Danish Blue.

Unit 12

Listening one Lambrusco – sparkling white; Bordeaux – quite dry white; Rhine wine – fruity and medium dry; Burgundy (Fleurie) – 1983, excellent red; House wine – very good.

Practice Model answers. You may disagree with these opinions.
1 Smoked salmon is a lot tastier than tinned sardines.
2 Beer is a little stronger than cider. **3** The hotel is rather busy. Half the rooms are booked. **4** Fillet steak is rather more tender than rump steak. **5** Indian food is much more spicy than American food. **6** A good soufflé is very difficult to prepare. **7** Hotels in provincial towns are a lot cheaper than hotels in capital cities. **8** French food is a little/a lot better than Italian food. (definitely a matter of opinion!)

Activity Sparkling, boiled, tasty, rare, hot, tough, soda, dry, grill, red, sweet, medium, cold, still, lamb.

Unit 13

Listening one **1** a knife **2** a glass **3** some water **4** a side plate **5** some French dressing **6** some cigarettes **7** the bill **8** a light **9** an ashtray **10** some tomato sauce

Practice **1** I'll get some. **2** I'll get one. **3** I'll get another. **4** I'll get one. **5** I'll get one. **6** I'll get another. **7** I'll get some more.

Listening two **1** napkin **2** soup spoon **3** fish knife and fork **4** joint knife and fork **5** dessert spoon and fork **6** side plate and side knife **8** wine glass **9** ashtray **10** salt and pepper

Activity Model answers: **1** Could I have some matches? I'll get some. **2** Could I have a knife? I'll get one. **3** Could we have some water? I'll get some. **4** Could I have some salt? I'll get some. **5** I'd like a packet of cigarettes. I'll get some. **6** Could I have the bill? I'll get it. ('the bill' = my bill: the one I have to pay, so we must use the object pronoun 'it' rather than the non-specific 'one') **7** Could I have a light? I'll get one. **8** Could I have a fork? I'll get one. **9** Could I have an ashtray? I'll get one.

Unit 14

Listening one **d** prawn cocktail **n** smoked mackerel pâté **a** Sole Meunière **o** Cod Mornay **k** roast pork **m** steak and kidney pie **g** Beef Stroganoff **f** Chicken Kiev **l** tournedos, **i** peas **b** French beans **p** spinach **p** carrots **h** ratatouille **e** roast potatoes **c** French fried potatoes **c** new boiled potatoes **j** Potatoes Lyonnaise.

Practice **1** French dressing is made from oil and vinegar. **2** Lunch is served from 12 to 3. **3** Dry martinis are made from gin and vermouth. **4** The wine is opened at the table. **5** Mornay sauce is made from flour, milk, butter, cheese and seasoning. **6** The dishes are brought from the kitchen on trays.

Listening two c, b, d, a, e.

Activity **1** Aioli **2** Orange **3** Tomato **4** Hollandaise **5** Bearnaise **6** Mushroom **7** Bechamel **8** Soubise **9** Mornay **10** Bolognese.

Unit 15

Listening one **1** They ordered 20 minutes ago. **2** It's overdone. **3** It's too salty. **4** The restaurant is short-staffed. **5** She didn't want cream. **6** It wasn't cooked. **7** There was lipstick on it. **8** It was in a very draughty position.

Practice **A** **1** arrived **2** booked **3** opened **4** cooked **5** melted **6** finished.
B **1** more expensive **2** the slowest **3** the best (irregular: good, better, best) **4** saltier **5** spiciest (most spicy) **6** tougher **7** the most popular **8** busier.

Listening two **1** dirty knife/get another one **2** twenty minute wait for wine/get wine waiter **3** no butter left/get some more **4** fish undercooked and cold/replace it (get it replaced)

Activity **1** i, j **2** b, d, i **3** m **4** f **5** a, b, d, i, l **6** g **7** c **8** e, j **9** e, h, j **10** e, h **11** i, j **12** e, h, j **13** k

Unit 16

Listening one Head Chef: roast meats, grills, stews, poached fish and pasta sauces. Assistant Chef: side orders, hot soups and hot starters. Pastry Chef: bread, rolls, croissants, hot desserts, pastries and petits fours.
1 knife **2** sieve **3** colander **4** ladle **5** wooden spoon **6** whisk **7** blender/food processor.

Practice **1** in **2** on **3** on **4** behind **5** with, on **6** for **7** into **8** at **9** at **10** from, to.

Listening two a4, b6, c2, d1, e7, f5, g3

Activity *Across:* **2** REFRIGERATOR **4** LAMPS **7** TIN **9** SIEVE **10** PASTA *Down:* **1** FRYING-PAN **2** ROLL **3** OVEN **5** MINCER **6** SAUCE **8** PLATE

Unit 17

Listening one **1** Roast pork and apple sauce **2** Roast lamb with garlic and rosemary **3** Veal ragout **4** Poached Turbot **5** carrots **6** celery **7** broccoli **8** sprouts **9** French beans **10** roast potatoes **11** duchesse potatoes **12** Chef's salad.

Practice **A** **1** must **2** must **3** have to **4** mustn't **5** has to **6** don't have to
B **1** Why do we have to blanch the vegetables first? **2** Why do we have to put the apples through a sieve? **3** Why mustn't we mix the lemon juice in the mayonnaise too quickly?

Listening two **1** c **2** g **3** d **4** c **5** e **6** b **7** f **8** a **9** e **10** c

Activity **1** c d f b a e **2** b c e a f d

Unit 18

Listening one £23.80p
Practice 1 immediately 2 politely 3 loudly 4 quickly
5 well 6 hard.
Listening two 1 René Leblanc/Mr Lubitch/He'll be an hour
late tonight. 2 Christine Burton/Mary Anderson/She'll call
before 9 am tomorrow. 3 Globe Travel/Peter Schmidt/Mr
Schmidt's ticket is ready.

Unit 19

Listening one 1 Mr Dreyton 2 July 10th 3 3
4 2 doubles 5 Bologna 29 31 05 6 6 pm (July 10th)
Practice 1 Did they arrive last night? 2 Did she speak to
the manager? 3 Did he telephone the hotel? 4 Did Mr
Dreyton call from Italy? 5 Did she order a dry martini?
Listening two Britain/Johnson, France/Duval, Belgium/
Janssen, Denmark/Landrup, Sweden/Eriksson, West
Germany/Schmidt, Portugal/Gilbao, Italy/Patrelli, Spain/
Gonzalez, Greece/Theodorakis, the Netherlands/Van de
Veen, Switzerland/Tell.
Activity Italian, Belgian, Swedish, Greek, Danish, Spanish,
German, British, Swiss, Dutch.

Unit 20

Listening one The first guest needs a taxi. The second guest
needs someone to repair the TV. The third guest is
complaining about the noise in the room next door: he needs
some peace and quiet. 1 DJ needs cleaning and pressing by
this evening. 2 Woman needs buttons sewn on a blouse by
tomorrow mid-morning. 3 Guests want to put jewellery
somewhere safe.
Practice 1 needs 2 needn't 3 don't need 4 doesn't
need 5 needn't 6 needs 7 needn't
Listening two 1 hairdressing salon/at the side of the foyer/
9–5, every day 2 travel agency/next to the hotel/9–5
3 exchange bureau/next to hairdressing salon/8 am–
midnight, daily 4 coffee shop/behind the lifts/24 hours a
day.
Activity

a 4	e 3	i 7	m 1	q 5	u 2
b 17	f 20	j 22	n 16	r 21	v 13
c 11	g 10	k 6	o 9	s 8	
d 18	h 19	l 15	p 12	t 14	

Unit 21

Practice Model answers: 1 Take the lift to the 2nd floor.
Turn left when you come out of the lift. Walk along the
corridor and you'll see the pool entrance on your right.
2 Take the stairs, over there in the corner of the foyer. The
sauna is just at the bottom of them, on your right. 3 Turn
right at the top of the main staircase. Turn right again and
follow the corridor around. 128 is on your right. 4 It's just
across the foyer, over there. 5 It's behind reception, just
past the offices, next to the bank. 6 It's in the basement. The
entrance is opposite the lift. 7 It's immediately in front of the
top of the main staircase on the first floor.
Listening two 1 dressing table 2 stool 3 bedside table
4 wardrobe 5 hangers 6 armchairs 7 mini-bar 8 chest
of drawers 9 TV 10 curtains 11 blind 12 air-
conditioning
Activity A – 3, 4, 5, 7, 12 B – 1, 3, 4, 6, 8, 9, 10, 13, 15
C – all.

Unit 22

Listening one 1 the railway station 2 nothing except the
river 3 the Odeon cinema, Lou's Department Store, the
Castle
Practice 1 down 2 at 3 into 4 past 5 on 6 Opera
House
Listening 2 1 Euston → Victoria line to Green Park →
Piccadilly line to Knightsbridge → Harrods Department
Store. 2 St. Paul's → Central line to Oxford Circus →
Victoria line to Victoria Station. 3 Liverpool Street → Central
line to Tottenham Court Road → Northern line to Charing
Cross → walk to National Gallery OR Liverpool Street →
Circle line to Embankment → walk to National Gallery.

Unit 23

Listening one 1 To visit the art gallery. 2 A modern art
exhibition. 3 The permanent exhibition, too. 4 A man has
fallen. 5 Call an ambulance. 6 Because an X-ray and
dressing for the wound may be necessary. 7 To go to the
chemist's with a prescription for another guest.
Practice A 1 Have you visited . . . yet? I went 2 saw;
haven't seen it yet. 3 Has Mr Tonini arrived yet?
registered 4 Have you finished . . . yet? Yes, we've just
finished (it).
B 1, c 2, a 3, d 4, e 5, b
Listening two 1 dizzy – lie down, call a doctor 2 broken
handbag strap – shoe repairers across the road 3 toothache –
aspirins, call a dentist.